The Cancer that Died of Laughter
Eyal Eltawil

Copyright © 2018 Eyal Eltawil

All rights reserved; No parts of this book may be reproduced or transmitted in any form or by any means, electronic or mechanical, including photocopying, recording, taping, or by any information retrieval system, without the permission, in writing, of the author.

Translated from Hebrew: Myriam Eltawil
Cover Art: Hila Dabi
Graphic Design: Shailiel Durani
Illustrator: Hila Dabi
Editing and Proofreading: Julie Phelps and Amit Pardes

ISBN 9781724086570

THE CANCER THAT DIED OF LAUGHTER

A HEALING JOURNEY WITH THE AID OF HUMOR

DEDICATIONS

This book is dedicated to my good friend, **Shiri Rahamim**, who died of cancer while I was in the process of writing this book. Shiri, who from the moment she received the bad news that she had only a few weeks to live, decided to go her own special way, full of infinite optimism and determined not to give in to statistics. She constantly had her special smile on, which affected all those around her. To her dying day she made every effort to make the world a better place and lived each day as though it were her last. She passed away after three years, against all odds. Shiri, you will forever be in my heart. You were and will always be an inspiration for a life full of meaning and essence. Thank you.

To **Ariel Tawil**, my dear and beloved cousin who died prematurely, but not before he had time to disperse infinite joy, love and giving, accompanied by never-ending energy wherever he went – a guy with a big heart that stopped beating too soon, but still has an influence in this world, long after he has gone. Thank you, dear cousin, for what you were and what you still are. Love you forever.

To Dror Wettenstein, a dear friend and brother, close to my heart, with an eternal smile and charming personality. Your pure heart, great soul and ability to face cancer with boundless courage, while smiling up to your last breath, are a legacy to the world. You have taught me the meaning of huge mental strength and how to be a good person. You are truly an example of how to live a full life, whatever the circumstances. I will never forget you.

INTRODUCTION

Several months ago, I started having back pains. The pain became worse from day to day. As a former cancer patient, the slightest thing causes panic, especially the thought that the cancer might recur. The minute I sneeze at a family dinner, my mother's on the phone, calling an ambulance. And then, just for the hell of it, she also checks the cost of graves.

Since I recovered, I've had regular checkups, which include chest, stomach and pelvis CTs every three months. All my results have come back clean, making me jump for joy every time.

When the pain became intolerable, I went to the doctor, who recommended a bone scan and an MRI. My oncologist received the results and, when he called, I understood by the tone of his voice that there was no reason for optimism.

It turned out that there were spots that looked suspiciously like metastases between my vertebrae. He requested some more tests, including a biopsy, in order to confirm whether it was a cancerous growth that had recurred.

My entire life passed before my tear-filled eyes. I crashed. The thought of going through the whole procedure again shattered me. I remembered everything I'd been through and couldn't function. I lost all my optimism, all the things I believed in that had helped me recover. Everything looked black and I just didn't know what to do.

Several years ago, I had cancer. I was diagnosed with Stage 4, which is the final stage. The next stage is where you meet God for a cup of coffee. Many parts of my body were filled with metastases. Nevertheless, against all odds, I won.

Apart from all the conventional and alternative treatments I went through, what helped me most was humor and laughter. There is nothing stronger, or more powerful, to eliminate fear and facilitate healing – and which helped me look the sickness in the eye and deal with it – than a healthy laugh to release all the anguish.

During my sickness, I wrote humorously about my feelings, translated them into jokes and performed them on stage. Moreover, I documented the entire procedure on video, from the funniest moments to the most dramatic ones.

Two years after my recovery, I staged a humoristic yet sensitive show called The Cancer That Died of Laughter, with which I tour the country nowadays. The show combines a standup about that period and video clips I filmed. In my show, the public shares my feelings and the influence this period had on my life.

Since my recovery, more than three years ago, I've dreamed of writing a book on all the funny events I went through during my sickness, a book in which I write about things I want others to know but have no time to deal with in my show.

I constantly put it off for different reasons: I'm busy with the show, I've things to do… and so on and so forth.

But this time, no excuse was valid. I had to laugh in order to survive this period.

During the procedures I went through, up till I got the results, all the while having to deal with the continuous fear of what my future would be, I kept recalling all the feelings and thoughts I had during my illness and tried to remember what was so funny then, and how it could help me now.

This book will not teach you how to recover. It isn't even a book about sickness.

It is a book about life as a human person in crisis, all the feelings during such a period, and the funny moments.

Enjoy.

ONE STEP BACK

Several hours have passed since I spoke with the oncologist. In a couple of days, I have to undergo a spinal biopsy. The result will greatly affect the rest of my life. It vividly brings back the first tests I had at the beginning of my sickness. At the time, I had to undergo a biopsy of my bone marrow, to check if it had cancerous cells. The results of the test were critical to my treatment.

I remember the trip to the ER, the needle they put into me during the bone marrow biopsy, the subsequent pain, and the nerve-wracking anticipation as I waited for the results. I try not to think about that and to concentrate on what I have to do at work. I go through my e-mails, but can't remember what I've read, who I should forward the e-mail to, or if I even sent it to anyone.

I get up to clean the house, but I realize that for the past fifteen minutes, I've been standing frozen in place with a rag in my hand, and the dust hasn't moved an inch.

I even sit down to meditate, as I have every morning since my recovery, but the only thing I can concentrate on is the tense anticipation of the verdict.

I work robotically, like a zombie, detached from myself and the world. I can't stop thinking that I may have to endure all that treatment again.

I try very hard to relax, telling myself there's no reason for negativity, that I shouldn't be having these dark thoughts before getting my results, that everything's going to be just fine. But the terrible pain in my back reminds me that maybe something's wrong.

I have to get through the night, and tomorrow I have to go to the hospital to prepare for the biopsy.

I've been through so much bureaucracy, so many blood tests, medical insurance forms, briefings and operations in the last few years that I could get a doctor's diploma.

It's seven pm. Thirteen more hours. On a regular day, the hours fly, but now I keep glancing at the watch and time seems to stand still.

What bothers me most, and is causing me extreme anxiety, is knowing. This supposedly minor issue makes all the difference.

Contrary to the first time I had to deal with the disease, I now know exactly what to expect. I know the exact processes and procedures I have to go through. I'm aware of the implications of negative results, how the illness will affect me, what will happen during the procedure, and what my future will look like if I have to repeat the treatment.

Even when I make a real effort to relax, my brain attacks long before my heart has time to respond.

When I got sick the first time and didn't know what to expect, I approached the matter with a great deal of optimism, humor, and laughter. I had no way of comparing what I would be going through. Every minute that went by was one more step toward a certain recovery.

That isn't to say that I didn't have my dark moments,

when I asked myself: *Why did this have to happen to me, of all people?* What did I do to deserve this? But these were only fleeting moments.

I try to recreate the feelings I experienced then, to try with all my might to stay positive in order to see the goal more clearly.

I succeed for several seconds, a few minutes at the most if I really, really manage to convince myself. Then, everything dissolves, and pessimism and frustration overcome me. Knowing what I may have to face is stronger than me.

This feeling is strange and unfamiliar; I've certainly never experienced it so strongly.

My entire life, I've been the funny guy, the joker of the crowd, not a drama queen. Humor and laughter even helped me overcome cancer.

So why the hell were these negative feelings suddenly plaguing me? I was, supposedly, a professional when it came to repressing pain and frustration. I was the master of joy, especially since optimism runs in the family genes, or more precisely, in my grandmother's genes.

***

I never met anyone as optimistic as my grandmother. She was the purest person I ever met.

In my earliest memories, I recall her always making a point of looking her best. Every morning, she'd get up, comb her hair for a long time in front of the mirror, and check that every hair was in its place. She dyed her hair regularly every month. I never understood why she did that.

As far as I knew, she never went to any nightclubs then, and I'm pretty sure she didn't have a thirty-year-old suitor waiting for her (and, in case you're wondering, she didn't have an eighty-year-old suitor either).

She barely left the house. Every few days, she'd go downstairs and sit in the garden to get some sun. Apart from her room, her armchair, and the bathroom, I doubt she even knew what the house she lived in looked like. I'm pretty sure that if she ever wandered into the kitchen by mistake, she'd need a map to find her way back.

Every morning she exercised and stretched to stay in shape. I checked all the sports tournaments, but never saw her name down for any of them.

It always impressed me. I was young and I got winded when I walked from my room to the bathroom. I didn't have the strength to pick up my bag, let alone weights.

She always wanted to learn more. Every day, she read a book from her library, as though someone would soon come to test her on it, or she needed the knowledge in order to impress someone.

The cherry on the cake was when, at the age of 100, she asked my mother to teach her how to use the Internet. Maybe she was working on a start-up and hadn't told us about it.

Apart from her knowledge, she was also wise, kind of like a wise tribal elder, or a guru. Everyone in the family came to her to pour their heart out and seek her advice. She was full of heart and soul.

The problem was that whoever came to see her felt they had to shout. There was something about Grandma that automatically made people think she was deaf and they had to scream into her ear, "*How are you?*" in decibels so high, it was like being in a club playing trance music at an after-show party. At a certain point, she really did become deaf, but that was because of the people screaming in her ear, not because of old age.

She'd simply sit there calmly, with that unique smile of hers, and enjoy everyone's presence. She was a wonderful listener and possessed a very special emotional intelligence. She listened quietly as though life was never going to end, and she had all the time in the world.

She was independent her entire life and lived on her own to the age of 96. When things became kind of insufferable, she went to live with her daughter (my mother's sister) and finally came to live in my mother's home.

You don't want to leave such a woman on her own. You want her near you all the time; you want to spend as much time as you can with her, as long as she's there. Besides, moving her to a retirement home would have killed her, physically and mentally. She died in my parents' home at the age of 101, surrounded by her beloved family.

However, that didn't mean she led a carefree life. When you reach her age, you're a bundle of problems. You start the day with a problem, and hope things don't go downhill.

1. She was blind in one eye. She wore a black eye patch and looked like a pirate. If she had the strength she'd had forty years ago, she'd have joined a band of pirates and stolen all the money my family never had.

2. Her son died of dysentery when he was only a year old, her husband died at the age of 54, and when she was 97, she lost her daughter.

3. She emigrated from Egypt, losing all her possessions and money, and came to Israel destitute. Not only that, her husband had to sell the only property they had in Israel for pennies because of his poor health. (In case you're wondering, it was the lot on which the Elite Chocolate Factory was later built. Oh yes, I could have been a millionaire today! Really, Grandma, couldn't you have held out with it a bit longer?!)

4. At the age of 96, she fell and broke her femur. When she could function again, she used a walker, which was attached to two tennis balls. Maybe that was why she exercised all the time? She must have entered a tennis competition on walkers.

When I looked at her, I'd ask myself: *How can everything be all right? How?* I didn't answer myself, of course. It was bad enough that I asked myself questions; did I have to answer them, as well? They'd have locked me away...

However, during my sickness and while undergoing treatment, I thought about her and suddenly understood, deep down, this amazing woman. It seared me, body and soul: she didn't fight life. She accepted it as it was, and viewed it as a temporary journey, part of something much bigger. The anger, fears, sorrows, concerns, and the losses – they were all legitimate. She was just happy to experience them at this age.

I realized that she invested in makeup and exercise for herself, so she'd feel vital and loved in her own eyes. That was the reason everybody loved her, because she was natural, authentic, and so alive, like life in all its glory.

My grandmother died two months after I was diagnosed with cancer. We didn't want to tell her about it because we didn't want to make her sad. We did everything to keep it from her, no matter how many questions she asked about me.

But I'm convinced she knew, that she understood. One evening, several days before she passed away, I looked into her eyes and it seemed as though she was telling me, "Everything will be okay, don't worry." Not a word was exchanged on the subject, and I'll never know if she really knew or not, but what I do know for certain is that, on that day, the expression in her eyes gave me the strength to maintain my optimism during and after the sickness.

I will never forget what she instilled in me – that life is just a small part of something much more powerful and mysterious, essential and deep, and that it's a pity to miss it.

So, thank you, Grandma Violet, I will love you forever.

LOOKING AHEAD

I hardly sleep that night. Even when I do, I wake up, look at the clock and realize that only twenty minutes have passed. I usually like it when I wake in the middle of the night. It's a great hour for creativity and my thoughts are sharp and clear. However, tonight, the only thing I can think about is living and surviving – thoughts that block creativity. I keep falling asleep and jerking awake. When I finally look at the clock, it shows 06:45. Time to get up.

At 08:00 pm I reach the hospital, look for a parking place, circle around, and find nothing. I'm not in a big rush to find a parking place. I pray all the parking spaces in the area will be filled, and I'll be able to return home and say, "Sorry, I couldn't find any parking, so put off the possibility of a recurrence to another life cycle."

After parking, I walk toward the hospital. Every step feels as though weights are attached to my legs. I reach the entrance. "You look familiar," the guard says, and the only thing that crosses my mind is, *I hope I'll stay familiar for many more years*. I enter, take a few steps, and everything comes back in a flash: the nurses, the hospitalizations, the treatment, and the nausea. I want to run away, I want to scream that it's not happening to me! But I have no choice. I keep on walking toward the reception desk. The secretary, who knows me so well from the period of my sickness, addresses me with a cheerful smile: "Hi, Eyal, how are you? You're here for your regular check-up?" I tell her why I'm here and I can clearly see her desperate look behind her reassuring smile.

I take the forms and head for the clinic where they take blood tests. About 100 people are sitting in the waiting room. All of them have the same look on their faces as I will have in several weeks. Waiting time is comparatively longer than usual, and I sit staring at the number in my hand. Suddenly, a woman in her fifties approaches me. "Hi!"

I return her greeting, although I've no idea who she is. She looks familiar, but I don't recognize her or remember who she is. She tells me that she's sick too, but I can't concentrate. Everything I hear enters one ear and goes out of the other. At times, I manage to catch fragments of a sentence. She asks, "What are you doing here?" I stare at her, as this apparently simple question takes on a much deeper meaning.

***

Besides the small and irrelevant question of whether I'd survive the next five minutes, the questions that bothered me most during the time I was sick were: What is my purpose in this world? And why am I here at all? And if I die, God forbid, what will I leave behind for people to remember me by? Because, before I step into the next world or anywhere else, I want to leave behind something deep and meaningful in this world. I want everybody to gather around my grave and say (if possible, in unison, so it will sound dramatic and heartfelt), "What a loss!! He saved the world just by being who he was. Without him, the planet won't be as good. How the hell will we continue our lives? The world's divided in two: before Eyal Eltawil, and after him. That Tsunami in Thailand yesterday was actually God's tears, because he just can't cope with the loss of this perfect creature!"

This is a fantasy that I keep running in my head and I make sure to keep it in there; otherwise I might be hospitalized for megalomania.

I truly believe that each and every one of us has a role in this world, some kind of skill, something special, a gift he can give to those around him that will benefit others even after he leaves this world.

What's my thing? When I was healthy, I convinced myself that I had enough time to think about this. Yet, as a cancer patient, I didn't have the privilege of time, and thus, found myself pondering the matter. Am I really leaving behind something admirable? Something that will make the world a better place? Something my children would be proud of? (Okay, so I don't have any children at the moment. I will in the future, so don't be petty!)

There are some things that are uniquely mine, and only mine. For example, no one else has a family name like mine to leave behind in this world. **Eltawil** – with about two hundred syllables and thirty ways of misspelling or mispronouncing it.

Nevertheless, is this really what I want people to say after I die? "Wow! He had such an awesome last name!"

I'm also leaving behind quite a rare collection of porn, which I saved on my hard disc on my computer under the innocuous name, "**Work stuff, do not touch under any circumstances, even if I suddenly die or the world comes to an end.**"

But despite those remarkable things, I felt that if I died I'd only be remembered as a cancer patient who fought for his life until his very last breath, and that the only thing people would say was, "Whoa! Did you see how he was blown away by the air-conditioning unit due to malnutrition? Awesome!"

I wanted to be remembered as something, as somebody.

Some important people in Israel have streets named after them, such as Eliezer Ben-Yehuda, Arlozorov, Prime Minister Ben-Gurion, Jabotinski, and more. It doesn't prevent dogs from pissing on the poles bearing their names, or youngsters thinking they're just names that the municipality made up by using random letters of the alphabet.

When people walk down those streets, they repeat their name over and over again. Waze knows and recognizes them, and constantly repeats them: *"In another two hundred meters turn right into Dov Hos St."* I'm pretty sure those famous people are sitting up there, congratulating themselves: "Great! A four-hour traffic jam in my street!"

For me personally, it's less relevant. It's hard for me to imagine Waze saying: *"For another thirty meters, keep driving straight down Eltawil St."* There's more of a chance it'll sound like this: *"In another two hundred meters, turn right into El...Alt...Uh... okay, forget it, just keep going. I quit."*

Some people leave behind plays, screenplays, or songs that make their statement: The Beatles, Metallica, U2, Shakespeare, Brian Wilson, Chekhov, Daniel Anani... (I know you have no idea who Daniel Anani is. Neither do I, but I'm sure there must be someone who goes by this name who wrote a letter or a song to his girlfriend, and I felt the need to immortalize him here.)

Some people have hospitals or entire wards named after them. People say about them, "I wasn't feeling so good and was hospitalized in 'Ida Sorasky.' Believe me, if it wasn't for good old Ida, I don't know what I'd have done about those hemorrhoids."

There are different ways to immortalize people, but the one thing in common is that these are all people who made something of their lives, left something behind – a legacy for which they deserved to be immortalized in this non-eternal world.

Not that I think that one thing's better than the other, or that one has to necessarily achieve greatness. People can influence others even through something small and simple, as long as it matches your specific goal. Who's to say what greatness is?

Okay, who am I kidding? This is exactly what I think. At the end of the day, I want an eternal life filled with essence. I don't mind continuously complaining that I'm alive instead of enjoying myself. But to die? No way. I just want to remain here forever, in any form, despite, or because of the hardships of life, even after death.

I'm convinced that Arlozorov and Ben-Yehuda would pass on having main streets named after them – even if it is free.

In our world, the most important thing is to be seen as much as possible; at any given moment; to exist and to constantly voice your opinion, no matter what. Millions of people don't know who you are and aren't aware of your existence. You're of no interest to them and they couldn't care less about what you have to say. Yet still, you must make them listen to you, otherwise you don't consider yourself important.

Is it really that important that I be remembered? Or is it

more important that I have the ability to influence as many people as possible, even if no one will know who I am and what I did? Who cares what people will think of me in the future, or if they'll remember me after I die? Many people not recorded in history have much more influence than those who *were* immortalized. I'd mention some, but I've no idea who they are.

When I was sick, I was surrounded by so many people who did everything in their power to help me and make me better: doctors who worked day and night and didn't see their families, friends who pushed aside their own occupations, family who poured all their attention on me. All this, just to keep me alive. No one ever heard about them or knows how essential they were to me, except me. Those angels are immortalized in my heart.

Nevertheless, and although I have an innate understanding of it, whichever way I look at it, I still ask myself every day: Is it enough? How can I make myself more memorable?

Until I find the answer, or until I understand what I'll be leaving behind in this world, I'm happy enough to leave myself, smiling, happy, loving, trying to be as good a person as possible, even in the small things. It's definitely more than enough.

For now, you must forgive me. I must resume writing something important, so that maybe, someday, someone will remember me for a long time.

STANDING ON MY OWN TWO FEET

It's my turn for the blood test. I say goodbye to the nice lady, making a real effort to remember who she is and failing. The nurse sticks the needle in my vein. I hardly feel it pierce the skin, but hear her say, "We're done," and calling the next patient in line. There are three skilled nurses drawing blood at the same time, and despite the sensitivity the nurse displays toward me, I feel like I'm on a production line.

I go out, collect the medical insurance form that I'm supposed to show during the checkup, and make my way to the oncologist for a briefing before the biopsy tomorrow. I'm scared of what he has to say to me, scared of what awaits me in the course of the day, and scared of the test tomorrow. I try, with all my might, not to let my fear manage me, not to be afraid of it and give it space. But the fear overwhelms me, sweeps away any good thoughts I may have, and obliterates my optimism.

I've been here dozens of times. I'm familiar with the situation and know this waiting room so well. However, my heart's pounding as though this is the first time. I'm anxious. I hear my number, but I don't get up. Maybe they made a mistake. Yet when they call my name again, I know there's nowhere to hide. I get up and walk toward the room.

I enter the room and sit down opposite my oncologist. Dr. Daniel Hendler has a unique sense of humor. When he laughs, his smile seems to take over his entire face. He's replacing my regular oncologist, who has moved to Toronto for two years. We talk, joke a little, and then he opens my file, which is on top of a pile of other files that belong to other people waiting for their verdict. He tells me what I already heard from him on the phone. My situation isn't good. It looks like the sickness has recurred in my spine. There's an 80 percent chance that the disease is back. Meaning, there's a 20 percent chance that it's nothing. My heart burns when I hear this, as though it's been pierced by a knife.

"But let's be optimistic," he says. "Tomorrow at nine am, we'll do the biopsy. It's important for you to be on time as this is a critical test that'll determine if the sickness has recurred or not. Apart from that, I'd like to get a CT of your stomach, pelvis, and chest, to rule out a recurrence in other places."

I thank him, get up, and leave the room. I'm in total shock. I keep hearing in my head: *There's an 80 percent chance that you're sick again, there's an 80 percent chance that you're sick again, there's an 80 percent chance that you're sick again...* I try to make this thought disappear, but it's stuck hard in my brain: *You're done for – 80%, 80%, 80%, 80%...* It won't leave me. I feel like screaming, "**Stop!**" but there's a lump in my throat. I have no words; my voice is mute. On the way out, I walk past dozens of people sitting in the corridor, waiting their turn to see the oncologist, and try to push away the thought that I may be spending a lot of time there in the near future.

I approach the exit and suddenly remember that I haven't peed for the last three hours and that my bladder's about to burst. I turn back to the toilets and stand before them. On the right are the men's toilets, on the left the women's, and in the middle is the one for the disabled. I stand for a minute and stare at the door in the middle and my whole body becomes paralyzed.

***

One of the "benefits" the state awards you as a cancer patient is that it recognizes you as 100 percent disabled. There are several perks: you receive a disability card, a disabled parking permit, and about 2,300 NIS (670$) a month from the National Insurance. Yes, yes, you heard correctly, that's the correct amount. The state thinks that cancer patients sit at home all day because they can't do much else, therefore this generous sum should be enough, not only for day-to-day living, but also to put aside some money for harder times, when they become, God forbid, 200% disabled.

The definition of disabled didn't appeal to me. Not that I have anything against disabled people, or that I think I'm better than them, or that the benefits I received wouldn't help me. On the contrary.

It simply bothered me feeling that way. True, I had problems and there were times when I needed other people's help. Nevertheless, as far as I was concerned, a disabled person was someone who was unable to function at all and needed those benefits in order to survive from day to day. Whichever way I looked at it, and no matter how I tried to turn it around, that simply wasn't my situation. I was justified in this. I didn't have to apologize to anybody, it was 100 percent legitimate – but, deep down, I was unable to accept it.

All my life, I've strived to be strong. I've done everything for myself, without asking for help, and now I found myself unable to do that, to say the least. The fear of being dependent paralyzed me.

I came across this feeling many times, but I remember one particular incident that happened one evening, while I was sitting in a café in Tel-Aviv. At one point, I had to go to the toilet to take a crap. The chemo treatments caused problems in my digestive system and I frequently had to rush to the toilet. Urgently. And when I say urgently, I mean *urgently*… At one point, I even considered taking my meals in the toilet to save the time it took me to run there.

It was critical that I reach the toilet as fast as humanly possible. When I got there, I saw that only the disabled toilet was free. Theoretically, I could have gone in without hesitation, but the thought that someone "really disabled" might come and find it occupied because of me, tormented me. I waited two to three minutes and, when no one emerged from the men's toilet (I swear I even considered going into the women's toilet) I realized that it was either go into the disabled toilet, or crap my pants, as simple as that. So I went in. After a few minutes (during which I destroyed the place, emitting noises fit for a building undergoing heavy renovations) I emerged weakly. It was just my bad luck to come across a Filipina care assistant, holding the handles of a wheelchair in which an old man sat. The two of them stared at me piercingly. I felt so bad that I started stammering, explaining and apologizing. The Filipina and the old man didn't utter a word. They just stood there and stared at me.

A moment later, someone came out of the women's toilet near us. The Filipina, who was with the guy in the wheelchair, asked me politely if I could keep an eye on him while she went in. Apparently, they weren't waiting for the disabled toilet.

I'm not here to apologize, or to say that I didn't use the benefits given me. Of course I did! For instance, the disabled parking permit was the best thing that ever happened to me. It was like a representative from the National Lottery of the Disabled called and informed me I'd won! This parking permit authorizes you to park wherever you want, and I mean *wherever* you want, however you want, and no one can tell you off or do anything to you. Even if the city tows your car and you get a fine, it'll be cancelled immediately because you have 100 percent disability and you have cancer, a winning combination that plays on humanity's conscience. And as a sick individual, this is definitely something you need. Because on top of being exhausted by your treatment, you also have to deal with infinite bureaucracy, such as picking up medicine from the drugstore, making arrangements with the National Security, obtaining medical certificates and more… parking is the last thing you have the mental strength to deal with.

The trouble was that, whenever I parked in a disabled bay, I felt bad. And not only that; I had a dilemma. On the one hand, I felt uncomfortable – using a disabled person's parking space – and on the other hand, I felt uncomfortable parking in the regular spaces, especially in the city, where there's such parking shortage. I felt like an asshole! And let's remember, I had a *disabled parking permit*, not a disabled asshole's permit.

It was all in my head, of course. It's not as if those around me made me feel as though I was doing something wrong. On the contrary! They encouraged me to use the benefits I was given, if only because everyone believes that the moment you get sick, you're totally unable to function. I felt it when a casual friend called during my sickness and asked, "Dude, how are you? How are you coping?"

I said to him, "Great! I just popped out for a walk in the park and now, I'm sitting in a nice restaurant."

So he said, "What do you mean? Are you allowed to walk alone outside and eat whatever you want?"

What was I supposed to say to *that*? "No, of course I'm not allowed. I usually have a Filipcologist (a combination of Filipina and oncologist), who feeds me inside my cage. She simply forgot to close the door of the cage, so I escaped! But don't worry, if – God forbid – something happens to me, I've got a chip in my neck and the municipality will locate me."

I have nothing against help. I simply think that those around me should show more empathy in such cases. Not pity, but empathy. A bit of tact could help, too. Not like that time when I was in a rush and decided to park in the disabled bay. As I got out of the car, somebody said contemptuously, "This is a disabled parking place, if you haven't noticed!" The best thing to do when coming across such individuals is give as good as you get. So I said, "Yes. I know. I have cancer, in case you haven't noticed." It felt wonderful to see him freeze in mortification, probably wishing the earth would swallow him, and hearing him apologize a million times. It was really worth the aggravation his lack of sensitivity made me feel.

So that's it. I'm back to circling around the city searching for a parking space, following the traffic reports and paying fines, and in general, reducing my quality of life by 50 percent. But I'm happy and praying to remain so.

JUST ME AND MY CANCER

I proceed toward the exit. My bladder may be empty, but my heart is full and heavy. On the one hand, it's a wonderful feeling, knowing that I can actually leave the hospital and go home; on the other hand, I know I'll be back tomorrow and may have to return many times in the near future. I can't shake the thought. I just don't want to go through the whole thing again. I start thinking about my options. I don't really have to undergo treatment. No doctor can force me. My life is mine, and mine alone. I remember all those cases of "spontaneous recovery" I heard about in the past, about those who cured themselves without conventional treatment. I remember just how much the alternative treatments helped me during my illness and how much they supported me physically and mentally and helped me recover – meditation, theta healing, acupuncture, food supplements, and others.

I seriously consider not coming for the test tomorrow and attempting to cure myself. Maybe it would be better. On the other hand, I'm aware that the conventional treatment I received in hospital helped me and saved me. I'm confused, and don't know what to decide and think. I sit down and try to reach a decision, but fear overwhelms me. I still haven't told a soul for many reasons. I have to share this with someone, but I'm afraid of being a burden and I don't want to bother other people, but mainly because I don't want to confirm — even to myself — the possibility of the disease being back.

During my sickness, the situation terrified me so much that I told everyone who was willing to listen, including the local postman! I was convinced that if I talked about it to people repeatedly, I'd finally find someone who'd tell me exactly what I had to do and not to do in order to survive.

***

One of the hardest things I experienced during my sickness was trying to understand what I should do in order to help my body and soul to recover. What were the right and most accurate options in order to survive? The problem wasn't the lack of options. There were plenty; they were simply hidden among a million other options, which contradicted each other. I had to reach my own conclusions regarding my choices.

My first basic error was to check the Internet and read about my sickness in order to understand it more deeply. I'm not saying that you shouldn't learn about your disease in order to have more tools to overcome it. Knowledge is power. The trouble is that the Internet is a tool that allows every random person to post whatever they want, whenever they want, without considering the consequences of what they say or write.

Apart from the enormous amount of information available, which would even confuse a doctor, the visual theories of what might happen to you as a result of your sickness are terrifying, and no one supervises their publication. You could die of a heart attack before the sickness does it for you! It removes all desire to keep going. This was one error I understood very quickly.

However, have no fear. Even without the Internet, you're never alone when you're sick. In order to find the ideal solution, all the "experts" in the world will be there for you: doctors, friends, acquaintances, people you never met, and people you never want to meet.

Every one of them has an opinion and wants to give you their advice and recommendations, promising you that this is what will help you fully recover. In the meantime, you have a splitting migraine because of the abundance of information, which almost makes you forget who you are and what you're dealing with.

People really have good intentions. There were a lot of decent people, like this sweet guy that I met in the hospital corridor, who started talking to me without my ever having said a word to him. I was walking alone, but apparently, I glanced his way, and he somehow got the impression that we were the best of friends. He started bombarding me with various information in an attempt to apprise me of the ultimate solution to my problem.

I've no idea how he knew I had cancer. Maybe it was sufficient evidence that I was bald, had no eyebrows or eyelashes, weighed about a kilo and a half and had a pole attached to my arm. I stood and listened to him because I lacked the strength to move.

He stared into my eyes and urged me earnestly to eat as much lemon as possible. When I asked him what made him so sure it would help me, he said that lemons have definite, proven mystical powers against cancer. He added that he was talking from experience, since his sister had been sick with cancer and lemon had had a miraculous effect on her!

When I asked him how she was now, he informed me that she'd died a while ago, after fighting cancer for three years. She probably left a lemon tree as her inheritance. It almost gave me the strength to go to the local cemetery, throw myself into the nearest open grave and cover myself with lemons.

I didn't feel contempt for the guy, truly I didn't. He was a good man with good intentions. I could see he really wanted to help – and lemons, quite possibly, do have strong mystic powers. I'm not denying that.

But when I related that story to a friend of mine, she said I shouldn't listen to that rubbish, and that it wouldn't help me, because my body was very weak. What my body really needed now was exercise. She outlined for me, *very* firmly, that I should do yoga, as it moves parts of our bodies that we don't use daily. "It binds the body and the soul together and works on breathing, and this is what you need now," she said.

Even though I didn't even have the strength, during treatment, to go from the kitchen to the bathroom, I decided to listen to her (one should make use of one's ears as long as they haven't yet dropped off due to the chemo). I tried it once, and it was once too many.

After the yoga lesson, I learned to appreciate chemotherapy and radiation. No more than two minutes in, I'd be gasping as though I'd reached the finishing line of a marathon. I found myself in unnatural positions that nearly caused me to dislocate my arm. I'm pretty sure I left a leg there, and my nose. The only good thing was that I was positioned opposite a clock, and I could see exactly when the torture would end. World War II took less time.

So – to whom should I listen? Friends? People who've gone through similar experiences? Professionals? When it comes down to it, they're all people with good intentions and some have limited knowledge.

The truth is that it doesn't really matter who you choose to listen to or what you decide to do. There will always be someone who has something to say. If you choose to go walking in order to strengthen your body, people will say that, in your condition, you should be resting. If you eat healthy food, people will say that you have to eat some junk for your soul, and if you eat junk, people will say that you have to clean your body. If you choose food supplements, like turmeric, they'll tell you it'll react with the healthy cranberries you chose to eat beforehand; and if you only eat the cranberries, they'll tell you that the turmeric was deeply offended that you didn't choose it and is considering suicide by jumping into a bowl of hot curry. In short, you can't win.

From all the advice I got, I chose, in the end, to become vegan and eat organic food, to enable my body to recover and clean itself. Before anyone gets mad that I dare preach Veganism and take a stand against animal abuse – relax. I've no intention of quarrelling or preaching. The way I see it, to each his own belief or faith.

Some people disapproved of even this decision, and I myself had my reservations, for the simple reason that it means giving up all your worldly goods, your pension and your savings just to buy organic products for a month. This stuff is *expensive*! When I went shopping in health food stores, I took along a security guard. But that was **my** decision. The most difficult thing is to make the decision, as it has to do with my life, and a wrong decision may end it. In the end, your decision forces you to act and take responsibility. It's much easier to listen to someone else's advice and, at the most, blame him after you're dead because of the wrong advice he gave you. I came to understand that nothing is right or wrong. Mistake or not, you have to make a decision and be at peace with it. It doesn't mean that I didn't listen to others and didn't drink lemon in quantities that would have been enough to kill all my cells due to over-acidity. I also meditated, had acupuncture and met with a naturopath who gave me natural medicine that helped me over that period – but in the end, the first person I listened to was myself, for the person who knows me best, understands me best, is most joined to me and my needs, and knows best what's good for me – is myself.

ALL IN THE FAMILY

When I was sick, some of the people who were hospitalized with me insisted on not telling anybody they were sick, not even their immediate family. I don't judge them, but it made me sad to see them die all alone. This time, though, I've decided that, whatever happens, I won't say a thing to my family until I'm 100 percent sure that the cancer has returned. I don't want them to go through this trauma again. I remember how they felt when I was sick, and this thought alone simply breaks me up. Knowing their child is once again at death's door will be the end of them, not to mention my super-sensitive sister, an integral part of my heart, and my brother, with whom I have such a strong bond.

I drive home, thinking of the people I'd like to share this with, trying to figure out who can give me the exact answer I need to hear right now, who will accept and understand me in the most profound way. I feel as though I'm on the verge of exploding, and I need an outlet. And then it dawns on me, and I remember who the lady was, the one I met at the hospital. She's an acquaintance of my mother.

There's no way I'll let them hear my news from someone else. I have a lot of experience when it comes to hiding critical and tragic news from the family; I'm especially good at disappointing them. And yet – not that way.

Several years ago, my brother was kidnapped in Colombia (it's true, I swear, I'm not joking). He was held captive for 101 days, and the day it happened, I was the one who received the phone call from the Foreign Ministry. I was in total shock (so much so that when they told me, "A guerilla organization has kidnapped your brother," my response was, "What? My brother was kidnapped by a *gorilla*?"). I convinced myself that he'd be home by the end of the day and everything would be fine.

I did everything I could to hide the information from my parents. The problem was that the same evening, while my parents were at a wedding, it was announced on the radio that some Israelis had been kidnapped in Colombia. I kept calling them every hour on the hour to prevent them from hearing the news by mistake. I brought a doctor home with me and asked him to wait in the next room. When they arrived, I sat them down and told them I had something to tell them. At the time, I'd been in a relationship for two and a half years, which made my father jump up enthusiastically and exclaim, "You're getting married!!!" He was smiling so widely, with eyes so bright, that my mother started grinning, too. I had to tell them that, not only was I not getting married, but that their son was in mortal danger.

I'm really stressed out, now that I realize I'd met my mother's acquaintance. What if she tells my parents that my cancer may be back? I don't know how to contact her, and I don't even remember exactly where my mother knows her from.

***

I must say, unequivocally, that **there's nothing like family**. Our unique black humor, the ties that formed, and the unwavering solidarity, were the main reasons for my recovery, and, for my family, it was worth living and fighting every moment.

Let me start with my amazing sister, Meital, who's been a kind of little mother to me. From the minute she got off work, she'd come straight to the hospital, listen to me pour my heart out, give me advice, take care of my smallest needs, and serve as a kind of conduit between me and the outside world. Even when she wasn't physically with me, she'd call whenever she had a free moment to check how I was feeling and how she could make me feel better. (The cell phone company built a new set of offices thanks to her phone bills during that period.)

When we were kids, I wasn't one of those big brothers who looked after their little sister, to say the least. At one point, she took judo lessons just so she'd be able to deal with me. I was a wild child on Ritalin, who went to a psychologist every Monday and Thursday (until my psychologist had to go to a psychologist because I drove him nuts). I was a problem brother all the time we were growing up, but she never held this against me, though I wouldn't have blamed her for doing so. Today, she's one of my best friends. One day, I really felt awful and told her about it. An hour later she came to the hospital with a guy she was dating at the time. It was their third date. (There's nothing like visiting a cancer patient in the hospital to get a third date going.) By the way, for their fifth date she brought him to my fundraising event – what the hell must he have thought of our family? I felt she really accepted me for what I was and wasn't ashamed of me, that I was really important to her and that she'd made me her top priority, no matter how high a price she might have to pay.

By the way, that guy… today, he's her husband. Apparently, the oncology ward's a good place for matchmaking.

My dear brother, Erez, who, during our childhood, also never received flowers from me, nor a massage every morning while love songs by John Lennon played in the background, was, nevertheless, there for me every second. Apart from the fact that he's a true friend and was always willing to help whenever I needed it during that period, he empowered me in a very specific way and wasn't even aware of the enormous strength he instilled in me. He was the one who filmed and edited all my video scenes during my sickness and acted as my technical director. It played an important role in my recovery. The decision to take a camera and film myself gave me something substantial and meaningful to do, instead of sinking into depression and just dealing with my sickness and its consequences. When I chose to document myself, I didn't know why I was doing it, I simply felt I *had* to. Afterwards, I understood that the camera gave me the opportunity to be an observer, an "actor in a play."

Apart from my dear brother, the camera became my best friend and went with me everywhere. To the camera, I could reveal my innermost secrets and feelings, some of which I didn't even know existed and found difficult to reveal to others. The camera became a sort of psychologist, only better: it didn't charge a hundred bucks a throw, nor did it end the session just when I'd ripped my heart open, leaving me with an open wound, just to have to pay again and spend the next session complaining about my huge overdraft and financial woes, only to have him nod sagely…

It was critical that my brother be there, because, thanks to our closeness and the security he provided, I felt much more comfortable opening up and being exposed during the filming. There was another, more practical reason that I needed him: there was no way I'd have managed editing the films without my brother, because he's a tech genius and the only one in the family who's any good at that stuff. He understands everything technical and the family can't do anything that pertains to technology without him. "Erez, how do I burn this data onto a disc?... Erez, how do I download this software?... Erez, how do I work this machine?"

I sincerely hope that nothing ever happens to him, and if at all possible, that he'll live forever (or at least die after me) because if he leaves this world, my family will regress two thousand years as far as technology's concerned. My sister will start sending letters via pigeons, I'll be drawing water from the well, and my father and mother will start communicating with torches.

One day, I was sitting in my parents' home, making a valiant and independent attempt to transfer the material I'd filmed on my video camera to the hard disc. I must have done something wrong because suddenly the screen went *black*. Everything disappeared; months and months of filming were gone. I *totally* freaked out. Everything I had documented was lost.

I screamed in panic for my brother (who was in the next room), as though somebody was wielding a machete over my head, threatening to chop it off.

He sauntered into my room and, with great nonchalance, succeeded in restoring the loss. (It took about 45 minutes, mind you.) While he took care of the matter, I calmed down. I realized that, besides being flesh and blood bond, I had a true friend by my side, someone who understood what those months of footage meant to me. However, most of all, I understood that, even if he hadn't succeeded in restoring the lost material, I was glad to have him.

Moving on to my beloved father, Benny. As a child, I always perceived my father as an all-powerful figure, whether consciously or subconsciously. He was an admirable figure who served as my role model on how a man should act. I trusted him to save me – to save the world – if anything bad should ever happen.

I never saw him cry and couldn't even imagine him ever crying, because for me, up till then, this was an act reserved for women and little girls. My father was always an easy-going man, full of humor and *joie de vivre*. He never made a drama out of anything (from whom do you think I inherited these characteristics?) but, during my sickness, I was privileged to see him for the first time as a vulnerable person. I'm pretty sure that he was always like that, but perhaps something in me matured and enabled me to see the whole picture. The "macho man" myth shattered, and I mean this in a positive way. He exuded a sensitivity and tenderness that, up to that point, I'd never seen him express so powerfully. It was also the first time I saw him cry. This taught me, whether he did it intentionally or not, that I, too, could break down, and that it was okay. This expression of support meant a lot to me at the time.

My dad and I often play cards. He's very competitive, like me. There's no way one will let the other win. Victory is all! During my sickness, we played a few times and when he won, he'd get excited like a little boy and boast about it. I didn't feel as though he was teasing me, but rather trying to tell me, "You're not sick. As far as I'm concerned, you're healthy and under no circumstance are you going to get special treatment from me, so continue fighting for your victories, and not only at cards."

I don't want to offend anyone, but my mother, the one and only Miriam, is top of the list. I can't count the number of times I thought about how hard my illness must have been for her. She carried me in her womb for nine months, brought me into this world, and I'm an integral part of her body and soul. It's amazing how, even after I emerged from her womb, she still feels me there, always, up to this day.

My entire life, there wasn't a pain, as slight as it may be, in my body and soul, that didn't affect her directly. When I felt a bit down, no matter how hard I tried to hide it when I spoke to her, by changing my voice and sounding carefree, the moment she saw me, even before I uttered a word, she'd ask me right away, "What happened? Everything okay?" like she's some kind of spiritualist medium.

Any time I felt under the weather, she'd put her hand on my forehead and say, with the assertiveness of a thermometer, whether I had a fever or not. I'm sure that, had I insisted, she would have told me exactly how high my fever was running. "39.4. You're burning up. Go rest, and come back in an hour and I'll take your temperature again."

Many times, it made her over-protective and blow things out of proportion. When I was receiving chemo and was totally exhausted, she came into my room and saw me with no socks on. She went ballistic and said, "Why are you barefoot? Do you want to catch cold?"

Yeah, Mom, as if right now, while I'm getting truckloads of poison into my arteries, my problem in life is whether I'll catch a cold…

But that's just how my mother is: caring and anxious, which often makes her pretty dramatic. Every little thing makes her jump and lose balance. Once, when I was hospitalized and my brother was in the room with me, he dropped a glass and it shattered on the floor. My mother, who heard that from the corridor, ran in a panic into the room, screaming, "What happened? What happened, is everything alright?! What happened!!?"

"Seriously, Mom, what could have happened? The Iranians shot a glass at us? One of the glasses decided to commit suicide and jump from the drawer? Apparently, the teaspoons and forks have been boycotting it for quite a while."

After I underwent my second big surgery, my mother slept in my room every night, huddling uncomfortably on a lumpy sofa in the corner of the room. One night, I felt horrible and asked her if she could massage my head. Of course, she gladly complied. I'll never forget the moment her hands touched my head tenderly. I immediately felt as peaceful as a carefree child. I felt myself returning to her womb (not that I have any idea what it feels like in there, you understand, but that's what I felt).

At that moment, I knew that, no matter what I went through during that period, she'd always feel me most accurately, most deeply – that when I looked deep in her eyes, I'd be able to relax and know that, no matter what happened, I could always depend on her and she'd know exactly what I was going through.

They say you can't choose your family, but I know for sure that I got the best possible option with mine.

SOUL MATES

I call my good friend, Lior Duvdevani, my soul mate. We've been good friends for many years now. We met at the Comedy Club in Tel-Aviv, when I was part of a trio performing skits, and he was part of a duo. We talk on the phone several times a day and can sense, from miles away, if the other is in some sort of crisis.

He answers the phone and I immediately tell him, "Dude, apparently I'm going to die. Any chance I can see you a few minutes before that happens?" He's the only one with whom I can talk so freely. He laughs and asks me what happened. I don't know how to say what I have to say, but the moment I tell him, he tells me to come over immediately. We sit in a café, talking and laughing, turning the whole thing into a kind of joke. It helps me.

We break the tension with the help of humor and sarcastic remarks. I feel comfortable and realize I chose the right person to pour my heart out to. He understands me, knows exactly what I'm going through, and is there for me. He takes an interest in what I have to say and, as time goes by, I start feeling better and notice, amidst all the laughter, a little tear streaming down his cheek. I'm terribly moved; it breaks my heart, and makes me appreciate our friendship even more. I don't tell him I saw the tear, and don't talk about it, but I'm a bit jealous, because I can't cry. From the moment they told me there was a chance that the cancer had recurred, I've been like a machine: zero emotion. If even a tiny bit of emotion rises to the surface, I repress it faster than the speed of light. I'm not surprised. I've been task-oriented my entire life.

When something emotional happens, I try frantically to find a way to solve it and only afterwards, in retrospect, do I realize what I went through. This is just the way I am. Otherwise, I find it difficult to function within reality as it is. Now, it frustrates me more than ever. With all the experience I gained from the time I had cancer, I should know how to cope. I should be able to cry or even break down. Nevertheless, I just can't. I hug Lior and leave, not before thanking him for being who he is. My conversation with him did me a world of good, filled me up, and I feel relieved.

I start driving home and suddenly decide that there's no way I'm going there, to be alone and stare at the walls, to be an armored hero who doesn't let anything penetrate. I call my dear friend, Dudik Mazor.

Dudik and I have been very good friends since we were eighteen years old, and – even though I'm absolutely straight – our friendship started with a kiss. When I was in the army, he rented a house with my then girlfriend, and she introduced me to him. The three of us got ready to go to a Purim costume party and it turned out that both he and I were disguised as women for the evening. (I *am* straight, I swear!) At one point, he said he had no lipstick, so I simply caught him and kissed him on the lips to share my lipstick. He burst out laughing; it was love at first sight.

Dudik is a very, *very* busy person, and it's hard for us to meet often. Yet he's the kind of friend that, even if we haven't seen each other for a long time, the moment we meet it feels like only minutes.

When I tell Dudik the news, he cancels all his plans for the day and comes to pick me up. We travel together to Jerusalem and eat hummus in Abu Ghosh. The scenery from the window is amazing and calming; I hear the prayer of the muezzin from the mosque chanting poetically in the background, but within me, a storm is raging. When Dudik asks me how I feel, I tell him, "Awful. There's no way I can go through this sickness again." He says, "Remember, at the most difficult times, we find within ourselves a strength we never believed we had, and you, of all people should know that; you've been there already." I stubbornly insist: "Why do I have to go through all this again?" And he replies, "Think of all the people who are important to you, and of all the things you like to wake up to every morning."

Every time I feel pessimistic and try to give up, he pours his optimism on me. His optimism gives me strength and faith. Sentences that could sound like clichés come over as precise and logical from his mouth.

We finish eating and are on our way back to my house. When we arrive, before I climb out of the car, I hug him and feel that I don't want to leave him, that his soul fills mine and that if we separate, I'll lose something. Before he leaves, he says, "Don't forget who gave me all my optimism, so it must be somewhere inside you."

The words my dear friends said to me today reverberate powerfully in my mind. I feel tremendously relieved from sharing, listening to what they had to say to me, getting another opinion from people who aren't as emotionally involved in the situation as I am and whom I trust.

I'm lucky that I know such good people, friends I know will always be there for me, even if, God forbid, the cancer returns. Whatever happens, they won't abandon me. Even if they fleetingly consider doing so, I have that secret weapon that every cancer patient has in his arsenal, which will make them think twice…

***

There is one significant thing about cancer that is good, that supports you and really helps. It's one of the most amazing things, nearly incomparable. And I mean, of course, the… the…. Wait a second, I knew what it was…. Goddamn, what did I want to write? *Argh*! I haven't the faintest idea… I remember! Oh yeah! Medicinal marijuana. Sorry about that. I smoked so much I've no more cells left in my brain.

It isn't worth having cancer just for this, but if you already have cancer, medicinal marijuana can really help. I've never approved of drugs, so when I was first offered cannabis, I was really against it. Later on, I agreed to try it and as time went by, I *really* became pro-drugs. Afterwards, I became addicted, and now I'm in rehab.

There are diverse and different opinions regarding medicinal marijuana. Is it worth using? Is it a medicine? Can you get addicted? I won't go into all these matters for two main reasons:

1. I am not an expert and don't understand these issues.
2. If I write bad things, my dealer may stop selling me medicinal marijuana.

From personal experience, it's certainly effective in certain situations, but you have to know how to use it and what dose to take. Apart from the fact that medicinal marijuana restores your lost appetite, helps blur a harsh reality, reduces pain, and calms your body and soul – **it creates a**

new circle of friends: medicinal marijuana mates – people you didn't even know existed, swarm round to your place and want to be your friend. I never had so many friends like I did when I was sick.

And if there's a fundamental fact I learned about medicinal marijuana, it's that it eliminates any inhibition, and not necessarily mine.

When I was sick, people stopped at nothing to try and join in the celebration.

The Recommenders: those who called me, asked how I was, and cloaked me with endless concern, sensitivity, and their undivided attention. They'd listen carefully, waiting for that moment in the story that would totally break me, and then, as if remembering "by chance," they'd say, "Hey, you know what could help you endure this? Do you get medicinal marijuana?" By the way, there's no right answer to this question.

If you say yes – you'll meet them faster than a tiger chasing a zebra.

If you say no – the next time you hear from them will be when the dinosaurs return to Earth.

The Pure Souls: those who heard that I received medicinal marijuana and offered to drive me to pick up the drugs from the distribution point, because I shouldn't be driving in my condition. They also made sure to mention that, since I had no experience with drugs, they'd be glad to help me roll a joint whenever I wanted, as well as be there every time I lit up, so I wouldn't get anxious.

The Dealers: those who knew how many grams a month I got. (For the sake of transparency, I used to get 20 grams, which is considered a small amount.) This information immediately activated their business acumen, and they'd approach me with various propositions, such as, "Man, I know someone who can give you a thousand shekels for 10 grams; that's about 550 bucks a month. Where would you earn that at a nine-to-five job? It's your decision, I'm just looking out for you. And don't even *think* I want a dollar from this. I'm doing this for your sake. You need it much more than I do. If you feel like it, you can throw a gram or two my way from time to time, just, you know, for the soul." I was forced to refuse those offers, since I would have no use for this money while I served my jail term.

Les Miserables: those who would request that I roll a joint for them, while playing on my conscience and telling me a heartbreaking tale about how the market was weak and everybody was trying, unsuccessfully, to get some marijuana. Apparently, had I not had cancer, there'd have been no way to get drugs in this country. Luckily, I *did* have cancer, which stabilized the market.

The Disappointed: those who were deeply hurt while saying stuff such as, "What? Dude, you get medicinal marijuana? Why didn't you say anything? Why do I have to hear it from Avi?" My initial response was, "Because Avi has a big mouth and besides, I don't owe you shit," but I was too stoned to remember what I wanted to say.

Everyone wanted to share, forgetting something meaningless and really irrelevant: that maybe I was getting medical marijuana to ease my pain. I didn't smuggle it across the Israel-Egypt border, and I didn't get it on account of my beautiful eyes (which are very beautiful, nevertheless), but because I was sick. I earned my medicinal marijuana fair and square; I didn't steal it from anybody.

Don't get me wrong, it's not that I didn't want to spoil my friends or that I don't love them. I really would have loved to share. It's just that trying to overcome cancer, while at the same time feeling as though I was disappointing everyone, didn't help me achieve my aim.

Although medicinal marijuana definitely has its benefits, I don't understand why there is so much enthusiasm about it. It also has its disadvantages, such as:

1. The name "medicinal marijuana" sucks. Why add such a depressing word as "medicinal" to something that's so much fun? It's not the right combination! It's like saying "orthopedic sex"… it doesn't feel right.

2. Marijuana makes you eat a lot, because you're constantly craving something. Chocolate, cookies, toast, a vase, stones – everything tastes great. I decided to turn vegan during my sickness, and nothing sucks more than having a craving when all you can eat is wheatgrass and broccoli.

3. The only place you can smoke medicinal marijuana is the place you cited in the license – which means, usually, at home. This is a serious restriction and when you think about it, it's absurd. Because it's not that when I'm at home I don't feel well and can't function, but the minute I leave the house I become superman.

4. Once a month, when you go to pick up your dose, you realize that you're not the only "genius" who thought about getting a license. The line's five miles long. It's so long that you start it as a sick person and end it as a healthy one.

5. You have to be very accurate with the dose you take. This marijuana is pure, clean, and contains no extra substance. One puff too much and you start speaking fluent gibberish.

So: if you ever decide to use medicinal marijuana, the most important thing is to remember to upgrade your phone to one with a lot of space for contacts, as you're going to be flooded with a lot of new numbers.

BEAR HUG

I lie on my bed and, although I feel a bit better about tomorrow's biopsy, I can't shake the thought that there's an 80 percent chance of relapse. It's 7:30 pm and the test is only a few hours away. My phone rings, and the name Orit Dembsky appears on the screen. We've been dating for a month now. There's an honesty in our relationship that both fills and scares me. On the one hand, I feel like she's my best friend, but on the other hand, I'm not falling in love with her and don't know if it will lead to something serious.

Lately, I've been having second thoughts about this relationship and when I talked to Orit about it, she told me she felt the same. The phone keeps ringing and I don't know whether to answer or not. She deserves to know, and I want to hear her voice. Something about her calms me and helps me open up. In front of everyone, I avoid myself. With her, I'm ready to be vulnerable. However, the last thing I want now is to deal with my problem. Also, I don't want to involve her if I'm not 100 percent sure about our relationship. I feel that it's not fair.

The phone stops ringing. I wait a few seconds and look at the screen. In the end, I decide to call her. She answers, we talk a while and I finally ask her to meet me. She tells me she can't meet me this evening because she needs to prepare an important presentation, but maybe tomorrow, if she finishes by then. I tell her I'd like to meet her today, if only for half an hour, because I don't know if I'll have time to meet her tomorrow; I don't even know if I'll have time to meet her in the near future. She's silent for several seconds and then she asks me, "What do you mean – in the near future? You want to break up?" I don't know what to tell her and once again there's a few seconds of silence. I start stammering and right away she asks, "What's going on with your tests?"

I try to avoid the question, but in the end, I tell her.

She tells me she's on her way to pick me up and bring me over to her place. I tell her I don't want to involve her and that I've no intention of involving her in everything that happens in the hospital. She tells me to feel free to do whatever I want, that I don't have to feel obligated, and that, nevertheless, she'll be there to support me until I get my results.

An hour later, she picks me up and all the way to her place she asks me about my condition, is interested in what the doctors had to say, and just listens, barely saying a word about herself. She's interested in me and in the information I give her.

We reach her place, get out of the car, and stand in front of the door. Then, she puts down the bags she had in her hands and hugs me – a big, comforting hug, which is just what I need. I start trembling and burst into uncontrolled tears. All the thoughts and arguments running through my head, such as "I hate to cry" and "I'm a man, I should be strong," are shoved aside when faced with such a perfect hug. I feel as though I can breathe again.

Later, after we go to bed, I wake up a few times during the night, but I feel more balanced with her next to me. Her presence helps me accept my neediness and makes me realize that I must accept that I need help from others.

Once, during the night, I wake up and she turns to me and hugs me. I stroke her hair and don't want this moment to end. I try to enjoy it as much as I can, but I keep thinking: *Why are you doing this to yourself and to her if neither of us are sure about the future of this relationship? And even if it turns out to be serious, do you really want to get close to her, not knowing what's going to happen to you in the near future? What happens if you fall in love with her? What if you hurt her? Why not break it off?* I'm trying to understand if what's happening here is right, if there's such a thing as right or wrong. I'm afraid of this oasis of good in all the chaos.

I keep thinking that soon, I may find myself, once again, without eyebrows, eyelashes, and bald, and what bothers me the most is if she'll want me like this.

***

I want to make something unequivocally clear to whoever's wondering or has a question about it: cancer patients also have sex. A friend of mine asked me once, dead seriously, "Do you manage to get an erection with all the chemotherapy you get?"

The answer is yes! I'm a man! I will get an erection even if, during the process, they dip my penis directly into a chemical substance, or if, alternatively, they cut it off.

Cancer patients have sex! I had sex.

Sex is proof that we're alive, that there's something beyond the body. Sex is an expression of connection, of love. It's a union with another mind and soul (unless you have sex with yourself). These are things you need when you're sick, because it's a period when you feel the most helpless and alone. And it's not the sex itself, but the need to feel alive and complete.

Sex as a sick person is very different from sex when you're healthy; there's no part of your body that doesn't hurt or from which a tube doesn't protrude. When you're healthy, sex is spontaneous. You change positions wildly as though there's no tomorrow, from the kitchen to the bedroom, through the ceiling fan and to the car. When you're sick, sex comes with an instruction manual:

a. Okay, come over here and be on top.
b. Forget it, I'll be on top, the tube's in the way.
c. Wait, wait a minute, I'll move my leg this way.
d. This way's no good, I've got the implant here.
e. Ow, ouch, not like that, that's where I had the operation.
f. Forget it, let's just cuddle.

As a cancer patient, I didn't have too many opportunities to have sex. In fact, I had sex four times. If I'm honest, then it's three times… and if I want to be both honest *and* accurate, then nearly two times.

The first time was with someone I met when I was sick. Surprising, but it seems that, for some people, a walking corpse is a turn on. At first, I thought she wanted me because of my money and due to the fact that there was a possibility I'd die soon, which would inflate her bank account a few millions. Then I remembered I didn't have a dollar to my name. This girl was a bit crazy, (not that I think that someone having sex with a cancer patient is crazy, definitely not). She was simply crazy, regardless. But who wanted to think about that? You said yes? Count me in!

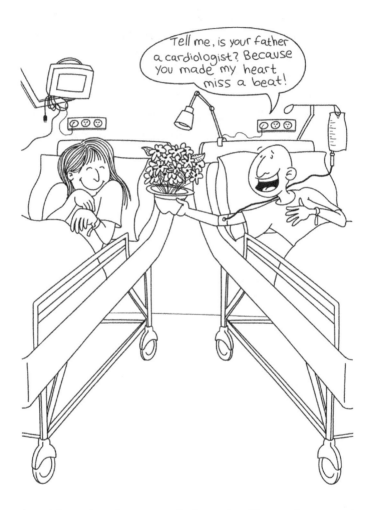

I met her when I was nearly through with my chemo and preparing for radiation. Before starting the procedure, my body was tattooed with blue spots. This was done in order to mark the exact areas to be treated by radiation therapy, thus eliminating the danger of the doctors irradiating, God forbid, healthy parts (as if I had any healthy parts left in my body). It was done just like a regular tattoo. To this day, I still have blue spots.

Once, when we were in an intimate situation, she noticed the spots on my body and asked me, "What's this?" When I explained, she stroked them and said, "Wowwww, they're so cute!"

In any other situation, I'd have accepted the word cute, even if she'd used it to talk about Stalin. But those tattoos? The last thing you can say about them is that they're cute. They're revolting, they're disgusting, they're not aesthetic, they're permanent, they're blue spots on my body.

Maybe, if after all the treatment, a tattoo artist connected all the spots, resulting, say, in a little bear, maybe then you could say they were cute. But those blue spots... no way. People usually ink themselves to express something meaningful:

- A dolphin, which represents freedom.
- Their children's names. (Like you don't remember their names?)
- Japanese symbols that embody peace.
- The name of your girlfriend/boyfriend to immortalize true love.
- A revered figure as role model.

I am 99.9 percent convinced that there isn't a person in history who ever went to a tattoo artist and said to him, "I want you to tattoo random, ugly blue spots all over my body," because they signaled all the points he would still like to achieve in his life.

The second time I was involved in a sexual experience, or more accurately, half of the second time... okay, honesty's really important to me... *one third* of a time to be specific! Okay, you got me. The only place it happened was in my head – when I was sent for radiation therapy.

I lay inside the radiation machine to receive my first treatment, and three doctors/nurses/care assistants – who the hell knows what they were, I was so focused on their beauty – stood before me. Their role was to prepare me meticulously for radiation. One of them had to place special shields, which had been prepared in advance according to my measurements, over the area to be irradiated. She made it clear that I had to lie exactly on the marked place, lift my arms over my head, and not move a millimeter, as this would result in the parts moving, thus irradiating other parts of the body.

The second doctor was responsible for looking at the X-rays of my body on a screen that projected from the machine to check that everything was functioning properly. The third doctor requested that I take off my shorts and then she put a shield on my private parts, so they wouldn't absorb radiation. When her turn came, she touched me lightly, by mistake, on the... you know... the place in which I react as a man, and I'm not talking about my mind.

She got flustered and immediately apologized. The first thing that came to mind was: *Why the hell are you apologizing?* I'm lying here, surrounded by three beautiful medical professionals, my shorts around my ankles and my hands restricted above my head. If we can forget for a moment the insignificant fact that I'm absorbing lethal radiation and that I'm a cancer patient, this could be a scene from a porno movie. This is the fantasy of every average man. So, of course, I wasn't angry at her.

I truly hope to continue having a great deal of sex in the coming years, hoping my penis won't drop off someday due to all the treatment.

THE POWER OF WORDS

Morning comes; Orit and I wake up in each other's arms. I look at her. On the one hand, I am so glad she's still here; on the other hand, the intimacy frightens me. I feel completely exposed. Something in me wants to run, yet at the same time, the last thing I want to do now is leave this warm bed and go out into the cold. I feel protected. She gives me a place to rest from all my habits. But I have to get up. She makes me a cup of tea and a sandwich and I prepare to leave.

We drive to the hospital. I'm confused, anxious, and tired; my feelings are a mess. I don't have too much time to think whether being with her is right or wrong, or how this situation makes me feel. I simply feel comfortable with her.

We arrive at the hospital and the moment she stops the car, I start rambling about all sorts of random subjects I would never usually bring up or think about under other circumstances. I can't stop talking, making up for my silence during the drive to the hospital. I switch stations on the radio and listen to music and drag it out until the last moment. Orit looks at me and simply listens, but at a certain point, she says, "You have to go, or you'll be late for the test."

As I leave the car, she catches my hand tenderly, looks deep into my eyes, and says only one sentence, one that penetrates my heart: "Good luck with the test. Don't worry, we're in the 20 percent."

Through her words, all my faith and optimism return. I really believed my end was near, that there was no chance I'd survive this, but something in her kind, confident eyes, in the simple way she said the words, and clarified things, and I daresay… I knew. It was as though God, no matter what kind of God, intervened in the conversation.

Something in the way she said, "We're in the 20 percent," assures me that I'm not alone and that everything will be fine, no matter what happens.

I get out of the car, still terrified, but with a feeling of health, vitality, and faith, which were lacking until then.

It's amazing how one sentence can change the world.

***

During the time I was ill, I was surrounded by so many kind-hearted people – family, friends and other beautiful souls who all taught me the essence of humanity. Every single one of them supported me and gave of themselves above and beyond to encourage me through the incredibly difficult situation that I found myself in. Dealing with cancer is no ordinary situation. Everyone who finds themselves in such unfortunate circumstance deals with the disease in their own personal way. Just like in any other life-challenging situation where the human defense mechanism is on guard, the wonderful group of people that made up my support system tried to give a kind word and a helping hand. Yet, sometimes good intentions are one thing, while reality is another.

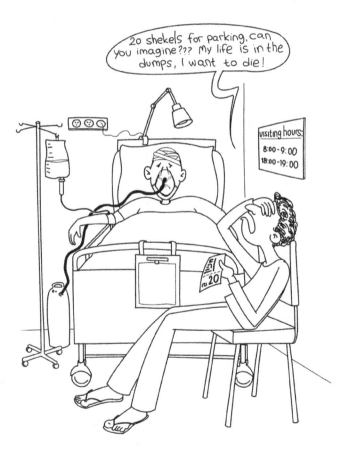

Here, I would like to thank all of you who have been by my side during my sickness and share with you some of the most tactless and dumbest sentences I heard at the time. (I didn't change them.)

1. **"Eh, so what's more radiation from a CT scan? The radiation you'll be getting during your treatment is a thousand times more lethal."**
   The oncologist, trying to calm me before another radiation-soaked checkup.

2. **"You know, you really don't look like a cancer patient."**
   A friend informs me that, perhaps, the doctors made a mistake and that I am, in fact, healthy.

3. **"I'm sorry I haven't visited you. I really don't like hospitals."**
   An unusual friend, who, like myself and other people in the universe, for some strange reason doesn't enjoy visiting medical establishments.

4. **"I can't believe how well you're dealing with this. I'd have committed suicide a long time ago."**
   A hospital visitor puts creative ideas into my head.

5. **"I guess I don't have to ask if I can smoke next to you."**
   A friend reminds me that I'm half dead anyway as he lights a cigarette for pleasure.

6. **"I'll need another form of identification; you really don't look like your picture in the ID."**
   At the height of my sickness, when I went to apply for a rent reduction benefit, the clerk doubted my credentials. Luckily, she didn't ask me to go home, cure myself of the cancer, and return with an updated face.

7. **"I have to hear from other friends that you're sick?"**
   A friend who learned late that I was sick, was mad at me for not announcing it publicly.

8. **"Don't worry, we'll get through this together."**
   A friend visited me in hospital and generously proposed to share the sickness and treatments with me, ten minutes before returning to her warm and pleasant home.

9. **"Dude, I'm playing poker. If my wife asks, tell her you needed me near you all evening at the hospital."**
   A good friend reveals the real reason why cancer was created.

10. **"What're you whining about? You're getting medicinal marijuana!! Believe me, God gives nuts to those who have no teeth."**
    At the height of my pain, a good friend of mine reminds me to thank God every morning for making me sick.

But, apart from what was said, the most important thing is that someone was beside me to say it.

PERSONAL ACQUAINTANCE

I get out of the car and enter the hospital. This time, the guard doesn't say I look familiar, but it doesn't matter because I feel that I know myself. I feel much better. Orit's sentence resonates in my head. My good friend Lior comes to help me, and just seeing him makes me smile. The people around me look like normal people going through a life experience (though a critical one) and will probably come out of it stronger. Me, too. Everything feels less awful. What changed? I don't have the time to think about it, because it'll soon be my turn. I go to the receptionist, give her a smile that says, "What will be, will be." She gives me the file that has stickers with my name on them, and I go up to the ward. On the way, I wonder what the doctor performing the biopsy will be like. What's his agenda? What are his qualifications? What kind of person is he? What does he look like? How much experience does he have? I know nearly nothing about him, except his name. It's important to me, because he's responsible for my body and my destiny.

***

Like every other person, I want some basic things in life.

1. **To be loved and accepted as I am.**
2. **To be appreciated for what I do and who I am.**
3. **To be recognized as the person I am, the sum of all my parts**.

I achieved the third of these in every sense of the word. There are few people in my life who got to know me so closely and thoroughly, without protections and defenses, as my surgeon did.

Surgery is a long process, both intimate and intrusive like nothing else. Therefore, it's very important that it's performed by someone you can trust.

Meeting your surgeon is like going on a romantic date. You want to get to know him well so that you can trust him and have faith in him during the surgery.

I was lucky enough to meet my surgeon before the operation, but I felt it wasn't enough, that the meeting was too basic compared to what might later be a serious relationship. I was excited, couldn't remember the questions I wanted to ask, and didn't really get a grasp of him as a person. In short, it wasn't enough for me. The level of intimacy my surgeon and I achieved during my first operation was incomprehensible; pancreas, spleen, gallbladder, liver, lungs, kidneys – everything. It was a great success. And when the first date's successful, you don't want to miss an opportunity, so we decided to give it another go and met for a second operation.

It was important for me to get to know him because I was recovering from a traumatic incident that severely damaged my trust. Before the first operation, I suffered extreme stomach aches for three months and almost every doctor I visited said it was a common reaction. When I got to a stage where I could hardly walk, I went to a doctor who sent me to have a CT scan, which proved I had a "little" tumor of 20 centimeters in my stomach. I don't understand how any doctor can miss a 20 cm tumor! It's huge! It's the size of a little person, and it's not something you can miss. What did I have to do to make the doctor notice it – enter the room holding the tumor's hand?

Even though it was hard for me to build my trust again,

my life depended on the surgeon and I had no choice.

Like every evolving relationship, you have to work hard at it. It's a long road and beginnings are never easy. So it took me a while to find the man who is one of the loves of my life and who saved my life.

The procedure started with me being hospitalized. They put a blue bracelet on my hand on which my name and ID number were printed. The blue bracelet's like the ones they give you at the amusement park; the bracelet allows you to roam the hospital freely, enter all the wards and use the "facilities" as many times as you want: CT, MRI, blood tests, operating rooms, etc.

After taking advantage of most of them, the nurse came to me and said that they were about to take me to the operating room. She looked at my medical file and asked me very seriously, "You're Eyal Eltawil, aren't you?" I said I certainly was. Then she said: "Tell me, please, what's your ID number?" *Are you freaking serious? Now* is the time to check my credentials? I'm undergoing surgery in a couple of minutes! You think I invented this identity in order to go through this amazing experience?

I gave her my ID number. She, in return, handed me a very fair form, which basically informed me that I hereby agreed that the doctor wasn't responsible for what might happen to me during surgery, and if, by any chance, they attached my eye to my nostril, or my pancreas to my ear, I couldn't complain, sue, or utter a word in accusation. This was, of course, if they didn't forget to put my tongue back in place, or if I died, as in both cases it would be hard for me to complain.

Due to lack of time and my desire to live at that moment, I skimmed through the document, and the nice nurse asked me, "Are you ready to sign the form?" as though I had any choice. It's not as though I had time just then to negotiate the fine points.... What could I say? "You know what? I'm not signing! I'll just hop over to see my lawyer and check the clauses with him, then come back to you with my reservations. How much time do I have before they take me to the operating theatre? A minute and a half? Great! I'll just get into my time machine and launch myself to my lawyer's office."

I signed the form.

I really wanted to meet my surgeon and exchange a few words with him. Apparently, I still had a long procedure before me.

The next step was to get me into the operating room, where I met one of the surgeon's assistants, a very nice Argentinian who inquired about my condition for a few minutes. When he heard I had a 20 cm tumor in my stomach, his eyes opened wide and he was so enthusiastic that I was sure he was going to say to me, "Forget the operation, do you know how many kilos of meat this is? Bring it over tonight, I'll bring the pickles, and we'll have a barbecue!"

Something about this nice, smiling, and charming man calmed me. Just as I started to fall in love with him, I remembered my main goal for being there: a date with the surgeon. I had no time for inconsequential love affairs or flings.

The calm I felt after meeting the nice Argentinian assistant quickly turned into indescribable stress when the anesthesiologist came along. It was one of the scariest things I've ever experienced in my life. The surgery was much less stressful than this encounter. A Russian man lumbered toward me (I have nothing against Russians, I swear, but just mention Russians and it sounds more threatening). He was about 12 feet tall and 300 feet wide, packed with muscles, his body mass the size of a thirteen-story building. He must have failed the auditions for the *Terminator* movie, decided a career-change was in order, and become an anesthesiologist instead. I was sure he was about to put me to sleep with a punch! The moment he approached me, I said to him, "You know what, everything's okay. I'll just put myself to sleep," and I lay down. However, I had some trouble falling asleep since the entire room trembled with each step he took.

At one point, I understood why they employed this particular anesthesiologist. He was the only person who could survive the cold in the operating room.

a. He was Eastern European.
b. You need thirty layers of skin to survive this shit.

I agreed to deal with any obstacle if only to meet the surgeon on his white horse, who had yet to appear. And then it happened. He came into the room assertively, with his cloak, looked deep into my eyes, made my acquaintance for about twenty-five seconds, which included saying, "Good morning," to me and the rest of the team and proposing we start with the operation. Not exactly the date I expected, but no one really asked me.

It frustrated me because, apart from the fact that I wanted to get to know him, I wanted him to get to know my personality so that later, when he discovered the rest of my problems, they'd seem minor to him. I didn't want him to wander down the corridors after the operation and tell people, "Here's the man with the crooked spleen. I've never seen such a weird liver in my life." *Excuse me?* You have a person with feelings here!

However, we had to start the operation, because apparently, I was only one of many patients he had to operate on today. Also, because the rest of the team was starting to get hypothermia due to the air conditioning and every little delay was bound to get them hospitalized because of it.

The anesthesiologist started by giving me an epidural and all sorts of anesthetics, and then something amazing happened.

I moved my hand to scratch my groin because of the tingling I was experiencing and then I felt it... in its entire splendor. It seems that the anesthetic caused my penis to develop a life of its own. I have no other explanation for what happened. (After all, the doctor wasn't *that* sexy.)

By now, I felt as though the relationship between us was

moving too fast. Never mind the fact that he was seeing me as naked as on the day I was born, but that was too much! I hadn't intended on getting to know him so intimately. After all, this was just the first operation; let's wait for the third or the fourth one.

Yet, despite my fears, I decided to trust him and, as you can see, I made the right choice. Even though I was fond of him, I decided that our relationship would be a short one, with only two dates. I still love him, but I don't think we're a good match. I'm kind of into being healthy. I only hope that he sees it that way as well.

TRUST EXAMINATION

I'm on my way to the ward where the biopsy will be done. I try to hold it together and maintain the new approach I adopted. It's a bit harder now, as the initial enthusiasm has worn off. Each step I take down the corridor brings me closer to my future, to my destiny. I see the sign pointing in the direction of the ward where the biopsy will take place, and my heart starts beating faster and faster, my thoughts start running non-stop and my energy levels decrease. I remind myself how I felt when I got out of the car and make an effort to keep that in mind and smile. Just before I hand over the forms at the reception desk, a nurse approaches me with a huge smile on her face and asks me, "You're Eyal Eltawil?" Automatically, my smile grows bigger and I reply, "Yes."

She takes me to a room and starts asking me a lot of questions about my health and the treatment I underwent during my sickness. She's interested in why I'm here and how I feel in general, what I do in life. She's interested in me as an individual, just like a good friend. Gradually, I open up and start with my nonsense, like going to a refrigerator full of frozen blood samples and asking if I can leave my bottle of water there for a few hours. She laughs. I trust her and, for a moment, I forget I'm about to undergo a checkup. It seems like another day in my life, the two of us sitting in a café, chatting. And then, while we're having fun, Dr. Eliyahu Perlov, the doctor who will perform the biopsy, enters the room. He's energetic and cheerful; all I have to do is look into his eyes and right away, I feel safe.

These people work around the clock, seeing patients all day long – patients going through unpleasant experiences. Some of these patients are frightened and a bit impatient. And yet, despite all this, these medical professionals maintain their joy, their vitality, and their courtesy. He approaches me, shakes my hand, and tells me to grab a seat. He shows me my vertebrae in the X-ray. He sets before me my previous X-rays and says that he doesn't want to promise anything, and certainly can't guarantee it, and only after the test results come back will he be able to say for sure, but from what he can see, it does not look like the cancer has returned. If my back was, indeed, full of metastases, I wouldn't be able to walk. There are only two suspicious spots in my lower back, and they haven't grown since my last CT several months ago. Therefore, he isn't sure they're metastases. When I ask him what he does see in the X-ray, he explains to me that the treatment killed some of the original cells of the bone marrow and in their place, cells of a different type and texture have grown; perhaps that's the reason for the suspicious findings in the X-ray. His voice is soothing, caring and tactful. As he talks, he looks into my eyes and puts his soft hand on my shoulder.

Then I suddenly understand... *this* is what's changed since yesterday! My attitude and that of those surrounding me. As long as my attitude was pessimistic, I heard the less pleasant things, the frightening and bad news. This is what

I absorbed, and this is what I projected. If I'm pessimistic and have no faith, how can those around me have faith? And it's mutual – when the people around me are positive, how can I not be that way, too? It doesn't mean, of course, that if I behave that way everything will work out, nor does it guarantee that my results will be good. But this way is much more pleasant, calming, and optimistic, and that's what's important. As I realize this, I get mad at my oncologist. Why did I have to hear from him that there's an 80 percent chance that the cancer has returned? These are only statistics. Plenty of people have been told that they have no chance of survival and have lived much longer than the doctors who said that to them. I, myself, have been suffering from bad statistics, yet I'm still here, alive and breathing. What right did he have to make me feel that way?

***

One of the things that bothered me most during my hospitalization was that every morning, regularly, doctors and specialists would gather around my bed. They were led by the senior doctor, who held my medical file and discussed my condition in detail. All the while, his calm tone and grave expression seemed to convey to them the following: "People, take a good look at him and try to absorb as many details as you can, because there's a good chance that tomorrow the only thing left here will be an empty bed."

I felt like a car undergoing its annual test and the mechanic was giving me a list of things that had to be fixed before allowing me back on the road.

"This is Eyal Eltawil, 31 years of age. We sincerely hope he'll reach the age of 32, or at least 9.32 am today. Eyal was diagnosed a while ago with Ewing Sarcoma and has been undergoing chemotherapy. If he doesn't die from the cancer, all the toxins we're pouring into his body at the moment might finish him off, and the chemo will be followed by radiation therapy and a bone marrow transplant to finally ensure this. After a thorough examination, this is the list of faults to be repaired:

1. Removal of the tumor from the liver
2. Excision of the spleen

3. Eliminate pelvic tumor
4. Opening of intestinal obstruction
5. No need to go on. We can fill a whole notebook, and we still have a lot of patients to demoralize.

On the whole, I recommend replacing him with a newer and better model. However, for some strange reason, his mother and everyone else insists on keeping this old and ramshackle one. If all of the aforementioned can be repaired, he'll be able to remain with us for a few more years, yet with quite a few problems."

As far as the doctors were concerned, I was invisible. I didn't exist. I was just a tool through which they transferred information. I have nothing against the doctors. I owe them my life, but they can be pretty stressful many times, because they operate on autopilot.

When you're sick, you're in their hands, you trust everything they do, and the only thing one can ask and hope for is that they're a bit more sensitive while they're helping you pass the test.

A BOOST OF ENCOURAGEMENT

The biopsy is performed under CT. It is a meticulous test, which requires careful scrutiny and is done slowly to avoid accidental injury to the spine. Once the needle is inserted, the doctor stops every few millimeters, does the CT, and checks that all is well, that the needle is in place, and that we're in the right direction. He constantly checks to see if I'm in pain or feeling anything out of the ordinary. He works slowly, takes his time, turns back to the CT machine again and again, penetrates with the needle a little more and never stops asking how I'm feeling, as though I'm the only person who exists in the world. His concern calms me and drives away all the bad thoughts that threaten to enter my mind.

At one point, I tell him laughingly, "Just keep going. The worst thing that can happen is I'll lose a vertebra or two. Better that than losing the patients waiting to see you today." He laughs and tells me, "Don't worry. I don't have any other patients today. I came in specially to do this biopsy after seeing your medical file." I can't explain how much his words warm my heart.

The nurse stands next to him, holding my hand when necessary, patting my head occasionally, and gently telling me that very soon the examination will be over.

I lie there, moving not one millimeter, knowing that the slightest movement can endanger my health and the quality of the test. On the one hand, I feel totally helpless, and on the other hand, I feel lucky and truly secure thanks to these amazing people who hold my life and destiny in their hands at the moment.

***

When I was sick, I came across some fantastic doctors who did everything in their power to help me. I feel I owe them my life. Unfortunately, I can't name them all, but I would like to focus on two people whom I had the privilege of meeting at Beilinson Hospital, where I was treated, and who were my biggest supporters during my illness.

1. Professor Hanoch Kashtan. I first met this special and unique man when I'd just started the process and before I even knew that my tumor was malignant and that I had a long way to go. At the time, I was positive everything would be finished after one operation and that my life would return to normal. The confidence he instilled in me from the first moment we met enabled me to create a dialog full of trust and tolerance with all the doctors and specialists that I met. His ready smile, his unique sense of humor, and his ability to project optimism while gently clarifying the situation in an assertive and very professional way, weakened every obstacle that came my way.

Professor Kashtan is one of those rare individuals who thinks outside the box. He adapts himself to every situation that presents itself, something that patients so desperately need at difficult times.

I don't have a bad word to say against him, apart from the fact that he's a massive soccer fan and supports Hapoel Tel-Aviv, and as an avid Maccabi Tel-Aviv fan, it was hard for me to accept this. If you think this sounds petty, you probably don't understand the rivalry between those two clubs. It's a derby! It's like Manchester United and Manchester City! I'd rather walk around with a popsicle up my rectum for an entire month than wear, even for a minute, a shirt that has even the slightest shade of red on it – which is Hapoel's color.

Imagine if he had to operate on me immediately after Hapoel lost 8-0 to Maccabi! (I know it's an astronomical score, but this is *my* fantasy and it's *my* book, so I'm allowed to say whatever I want!) Who could promise me he wouldn't leave a Hapoel scarf in my abdomen as a souvenir!?

I met him before my first surgery. He was chosen randomly by the hospital to operate on me, a marvelous choice that made me as happy as can be. I came to him with terrible pains in my abdomen due to the 20-cm tumor growing in it – a huge tumor, about which I'm sure 99 percent of the doctors I might have consulted would have panicked, insisting I have the operation right there and then, in their office, just in case I didn't survive the next few steps to the door.

I made it clear to him that it was important for me to try and make the tumor disappear with the help of alternative treatments. I truly believed then, and still believe today, that I'm in control of my health. I believe with all my heart that every sickness I endure starts, first and foremost, in my soul as a result of unresolved issues within myself. Of course, I'd never tell anyone not to undergo conventional treatments, or that they're in any way to blame for being sick, God forbid! It's just that the support of those alternative treatments can definitely help. They helped me a great deal during my treatment and help me to this day.

Nearly every other doctor would have said **NO** without giving it another thought, while reserving a place for me in an asylum and ensuring I remained in isolation under lock and key until my last day – which, in my condition, would be at the most two months away.

However, Professor Kashtan pored over the documents and X-rays I brought him, then looked up at me and said calmly, "I think it won't do much harm to wait a bit longer. Anyway, the date of the operation is only a month from now, so there should be no problem. You have three weeks, after which we'll do a CT. If the tumor gets smaller, we'll continue doing things your way. If not, give me your word that we'll operate immediately. Agreed?"

I have no words to describe how happy I felt and how much I trusted him right then. Of course I agreed and began the process. I meditated every day, and started a treatment de-

scribed in Brandon Bays' book *The Journey*, which is based on dealing with profound childhood experiences, and the emotional decomposition of body cells. I did theta-healing treatments and many other empowering treatments. I felt wonderful. Every night I would go to bed calm and fall asleep, but in the middle of the night I'd wake up with dreadful pains in my stomach, worse than those I'd experienced before starting the alternative treatments. In the end, the pain got the better of me and after two weeks, I phoned Professor Kashtan and told him that I had to have the operation because I was in terrible pain. He confirmed the date of the surgery and I knew, without any doubt, that I could entrust my body to his hands.

Then, something amazing happened. When the surgery was over, he came to me and told me two things, which sent shivers through my body:

1. **I've been a surgeon for a long time, but I never saw such a huge tumor. Where the hell did you get it from?!**
2. **The entire tumor was shredded. It was really strange.**

I'll never know the real reason why the tumor was shredded, but I think that the terrible pain I felt every night during the alternative treatments was the reason for that. I felt that every cell in my body was active, operating places in my soul that I never had the courage to confront, which finally resulted in the growth of the tumor.

Perhaps if I'd continued the alternative treatments for several more days, I would have achieved better results that might have enabled me to forego surgery. I don't know. What I do know for sure is that this great man removed the tumor entirely, cleaned my stomach cavity, and at the same time let me clean my soul.

So thank you, dear Professor Kashtan, you are in my heart forever. And may you suffer defeat in the next cup match… amen. I love you, Maccabi!!!

2. Reuven the masseur – The second angel I met was Reuven the masseur. During my sickness, a regular massage was one of the things that calmed, pampered, and supported my body and soul more than anything. The human touch I craved so badly lovingly dissolved all the toxins that penetrated my cells and relieved all the pain my body had accumulated.

I am addicted to massage and when I say addicted, I mean *addicted*. I'm ready for a massage any time, in any way or form – standing, sitting, lying down, driving, in hospital, before surgery, during surgery, at a funeral, at my funeral – always!

I immediately submit, like a little kitten who starts purring the second you start petting him, and I make noises like a refrigerator in the middle of the night. I simply lose touch with my mind, start floating and forget about the whole world and all its problems. When I get a massage, you can tell me anything and I'll agree. "What was that? You want me to go into partnership with you in a start-up of aliens that'll produce dark-pink bananas? And all you need from me is a million dollars? Grab the checkbook from my bag and take two million." I'll give anything for a good massage and I don't care who does it for me; it can be a serial killer holding an ax in one hand as the other hand presses my shoulders. As far as I'm concerned, the ideal death would be whilst having a massage!

When I was hospitalized in the Beilinson Hospital, I used to go down to one of the basement level floors, to the

Alternative Medicine Ward, to meet Reuven Baron. Besides being one of the best masseurs I've ever met, and apart from the fact that I'd leave his room so calm that I'd feel as though I was floating, I admired this man for who he was.

Reuven is not a standard masseur; he's almost entirely blind. The first time I went to see him, I wasn't aware of that. He doesn't walk around with a sign hanging around his neck proclaiming blindness. The truth is that, had he not told me, I wouldn't have guessed. He was so sure of himself, so calm, and unapologetic.

The massage was so good! He felt precisely every spot on my body, and the moment I felt pain somewhere, his hands were already there. We started talking (one of my problems in life is that even while having a massage, I find it hard to shut my mouth), and while enjoying the pressure of his hands, he casually told me about his disability.

He told me, ever so humorously, about all the difficulties involved. Once, he asked somebody to help him cross the road. He made the request many times, yet never received an answer. After asking repeatedly, he realized he was talking to a traffic light.

Another time he saw a cat on the sidewalk and started petting him, while meowing softly, when all of a sudden, a phone company technician jumped up and shouted at him, "What are you doing?" Apparently, the "cat" was his foot, and Reuven's meowing had scared him.

The first thought that crossed my mind was: who wants to live that way? Then, I mustered the courage to ask him, "How do you feel about it?" With his typical humor, he replied, "Thank God, it's getting worse from day to day," and laughed. I was amazed. I felt he saw much more than me. Life had given this man such a big challenge to deal with, yet he refused to complain. Instead, he was extremely active and accepting. I understood this even more profoundly when he told me that he hadn't been born blind, but that his eyesight had deteriorated over the years, which meant that he knew what he was missing. I asked him what he did every day when he finished work, and he replied, "I go home to my Italian wife. We've been together for eleven years. (*Italian*! I can see perfectly and I've *never* been with an Italian!) We go out in the evening, hang out with our four children from previous marriages (wow, what an achievement), meet our five grandchildren (would you believe it?), and I go jogging three times a week…." I was sure he was joking and I burst out laughing, but it turned out he was dead serious. "How?" I asked him. He explained to me that in the past, he'd jogged during the day and the shadows he saw directed him. "From time to time, I'd take short breaks when I met a pole or obstacle that bothered me on the way," and then he added laughing, "I'm training now for a triathlon. I run accompanied by another runner who's attached to me by a rubber band."

All these things were related to me by a 61-year-old man (at the time), who had experienced enough things in life and was entitled to say at one point, "That's enough, I've worked pretty hard, achieved a lot, I deserve to rest." Not him. At a certain point, when I finally shut up, I thought about myself, 31 years old, going through the most difficult phase in my life, which would end someday, enabling me to return to my regular life, and I decided that I wouldn't complain. I wouldn't give up, and I certainly wouldn't indulge in self-pity. I would win, come what may.

At the end of my first massage, when I left, he said to me, "If you want to make an appointment, don't send me a text. It might delay the process a little." I laughed. I went home and made many more appointments, by phone of course.

I gradually started to realize that I went to him, not for the massage, but to hear him talk and to absorb his energy, which gave me strength, supported my belief in life and recovery, and showed me another unique perspective on how to deal with cancer.

So, thank you so much, Reuven. Thanks to you, I see life in a more positive way.

A PARTNER FOR THE ROAD AHEAD

The biopsy is nearly over. The doctor leaves the room, makes his last trip to the CT machine, checks if any problems have popped up, and then returns to me. He removes the needle from my back and informs me that the biopsy has been successfully taken and that, within two-and-a-half weeks, we'll receive results telling us whether the tumor is malignant or not. The moment I hear those words "malignant tumor," I want to get up and run away. My feeling of well-being evaporates. I get up from the bed, say thank you very much, and stand up. Or, to be more precise, I try to stand… but I've forgotten one small and relevant detail, which is that an injection in the spine weakens and numbs the feet.

I get up, and immediately crumple. The doctor catches me a second before I crash. He brings me a wheelchair, tells me to relax and rest, and an orderly takes me out to the corridor. I'm stressed out as I sit there. I want to stand up and check if everything is fine. I'm scared that my spine's been damaged and that I'll remain disabled for the rest of my life, and that my fall is a result of irreparable damage to my feet or my back. The doctor comes by a few times and makes it clear I have nothing to worry about. These are the aftereffects of the biopsy, he tells me, but I'm still not convinced. Only half an hour later, when I can finally stand on my own two feet and walk away, do I calm down. All of a sudden, each step isn't taken for granted. I feel as though my body has returned to me.

I thank the doctor and the nurse more times than the days of the year and I still feel it's not enough. I go down to one of the candy stores, buy chocolates, write them a card, and go back to give it to them. I also invite them to come and see my show The Cancer That Died of Laughter and they promise to make every effort to come.

I go back to the ward to return my medical file. I start feeling a pain in my back because of the biopsy, but the effect of the anesthetic and the adrenaline push me on and fill me with energy. In the corridor, I hear a familiar voice calling my name. I turn around and see the oncologist. My body freezes and tenses, and rage fills me. I mentally prepare a massive dress down. As he approaches me, I get ready to shoot with all my might. Every step he takes toward me just makes me angrier. When he reaches me, he has a huge smile on his face as he asks, "Did you hear the doctor's news? There's a good chance that what they saw on your back aren't metastases and that you're entirely healthy. Isn't that great!" He's so happy, like a little boy who's been given a toy. He takes this personally and, in the space of a second, all my anger turns into compassion and love. I remember that, despite the fact that I want him to be a "superman doctor" who'll save me, who'll always know what's right, who'll adjust to my will and be as sensitive as possible, he is, first and foremost, just like me and like everybody else:

a person with feelings.

He treats dozens of patients every day, and when you do so much good for others, it's only natural that you occasionally make mistakes, or that you won't always be exactly what each person expects you to be.

I think about everything he's done for me to this day, of all the times I needed forms and certifications and he sent them to me, how he's always available to take my phone calls and answer all my questions, how he always takes care of every detail to keep me healthy, feeling good, and happy. He is one of the people I most admire and, in the end, he did his work as he saw fit, and told me the facts as he saw them.

I share my feelings with him, explaining how much I appreciate everything he does, but that for me life is much more than dry facts.

I tell him that, although I'm aware that as a doctor, it's his duty to inform me of what might happen, as far as I'm concerned, the question is how much information is needed and how that information is relayed.

I explain to him that, even when I come pessimistic, faithless, and frightened, I want to know that I've come to a place that can accept me, where I can calm down, no matter how bad the news. I expect the most experienced person at the time to be the responsible adult.

One look is sufficient to convey what we mean to each other and that he understood what I said. I hug him, look deep into his eyes, and am thankful that I have such an oncologist.

***

A great many doctors treated me when I had cancer. Most were kind, sensitive, and dedicated to their work, or at least they tried to be. But there was one time when I received treatment that I'll never forget. The standard of professionalism and sensitivity was above and beyond. I felt like a VIP patient.

Every three months or so, I'd suffer from a bowel obstruction. In short, it means that the rectum gets obstructed. It causes stomach aches and in order to administer fluids, they stick a gastric tube, via your nose, straight into your stomach.

Some background on the human body: we have the small intestine that's responsible for the absorption of the food ingredients; the colon, which connects the small intestine to the anus and is responsible for the absorption of the liquids; and the blind intestine that doesn't give a shit, because it can't see anything anyway. When this whole construction goes crazy, you're doomed.

That's exactly when you learn to appreciate the little things in life! I never felt so much appreciation and gratitude for a lump of shit coming out of my body. If I had to choose between a million dollars in cash or two minutes in the bathroom, I've no doubt I'd choose the latter. On second thoughts, maybe I'd take the million dollars, buy myself a new ass, and spend the rest.

No doctor or plumber can do a thing except wait for the blockage to clear. And if that doesn't happen after a day or two, one has to undergo surgery because the body can't accumulate unlimited trash. But before you can dispose of the "garbage" that has accumulated in your intestines, a little something has to happen: **a fart!** Even a tiny one, which you can hardly hear, even if it just sounds like a whisper of the wind, is the perfect sign that the blockage has opened.

The greatest of people are made famous by little things. Never has such a big team of doctors entered my room so many times a day, conducting frequent morning meetings around my bed, constantly asking how I felt, expressing such concern and dedication – all this in order to hear if I had succeeded in farting! The number of times I heard them ask, "Well? Did you pass wind? Any luck?" all of them deadly serious, is equivalent to the number of times I farted in my entire life! And let me just point out that white beans are my favorites.

Had they known, before they went to med school, that they were going to waste seven years of school, meet endless patients, conduct hundreds of tests, exams, and hours of treatment, and in general, invest their entire lives in something they believed in, only to check if one person had managed to fart, I'm sure they'd have chosen another profession.

Nothing in the world was more important. The doctors stood around my bed, alert to any forthcoming fart. I'm pretty sure that had a doctor entered the room just then, screaming in panic, "Come urgently! There's someone in the corridor who has no pulse!" they'd have replied, "Where are your priorities? This guy has to fart first, and then we'll be free to take care of your nonsense."

I couldn't stop thinking of all the married men at home who probably thought: *If my wife praised me every time I farted, our relationship would be so great…*

The greater your feeling of stress because of your inability to live up to the doctors' expectations, the greater your feeling of freedom and happiness the moment you succeed. I felt as though I'd won the lottery. I was so happy, I called to whoever would listen and told them, "I farted!" At one point, the woman at the other end of the line said to me, "Sir, with all due respect, this is the Customer Service Department of a car rental agency."

When I come to think of it, not everybody was happy about it. A fart that erupts after three fart-less days could neutralize the chemo – not only mine, but that of all the patients in the building. After I finally farted, the nurses turned green, the doctors worked for weeks with the help of oxygen tanks, there were cracks in the walls, and chaos all around. I'm pretty sure my fart caused an ecological disaster somewhere in the world.

If there's something that increases your chances of surviving cancer, it's the devoted, caring, sensitive, and professional doctors who do their job. So many toxic substances enter your body that it's essential to have someone human to balance it. By the way, that's one thing that I've never understood; doctors treating cancer with substances that may cause another kind of cancer. It's crazy. It's like going to the doctor and telling him, "Doctor, I'm coughing like crazy. What should I do?" And he tells you, "I'm prescribing you a packet of Marlboros; smoke three packets a day and you'll be cured."

As a patient, you want your doctor to be the best and the most professional because, whichever way you look at it, your life depends on him. You'll do everything to forget that he's a human being, like you, capable of making mistakes. Unfortunately, I happened to come across doctors that didn't make it possible for me to avoid such thoughts.

One day, after an invasive test, I got the results. I sat with the doctor, who easily deciphered the results from a page that was full of numbered combinations, letters, and formulae that wouldn't have shamed one of Da Vinci's codes. I've no idea how she understood anything. In my opinion, Albert Einstein would have looked at that page and said, "Gimme a break! How am I supposed to solve this shit? I need a career change..." I told her, "Listen, you must be a genius. How the hell do you remember all those formulae?" She raised her head from the pages and said, "It's not simple. During my training there were a lot of exams, and I had to take some of them several times before I passed. It was tons of material, and I have a short memory."

That's just about the last thing you want to hear from a doctor who holds your destiny in her hands. Take a tutor, if necessary, or switch your brain with one that has a better memory. I imagined her as part of a team performing emergency surgery on me. "Okay, Mr. Chief Surgeon, I've removed the heart, but I don't understand why I can't join it back to the rectum…?"

For instance, during one of my treatments, while the nurse was holding the chemo bag containing all the toxins, it slipped from her hands in a moment of distraction. I said, "Be careful." She just laughed and said, "Some days I seem to drop everything!"

What? No! Then call me here on the other days. I want to live! Today it's the bag, tomorrow it'll be my kidney.

In future, if I need medical attention, I'd like to receive the same kind of attention I had from all those doctors during my bowel obstruction.

FILLING THE VOID

Orit calls and asks if she should come and pick me up. Even though I want her soothing presence, I insist on taking a cab and being by myself. My brain is about to burst. I reach home, throw my bag on the floor, and lie on the bed. Just then, it's the most amazing feeling in the world. The next thing I remember is waking up at 5.00 am. All the tension and stress of the biopsy resulted in nine hours' sleep.

I try to go back to sleep again, but I can't. My thoughts keep me awake, as well as the pain from the biopsy. I get up and take a shower. It's not a regular shower, but one that washes out all the tension. Every drop of water flowing over my body penetrates my soul and cleans me. I remain there until the last drop of hot water and only then come out. I make myself a cup of tea, sit, and stare at the room, doing nothing. It's not something I take for granted, sitting peacefully in the silence without any chaos and drama. I listen to the quiet outside and it neutralizes the noises in my head. Being alone usually stresses me; I immediately try to escape my own company. Give me anybody or anything, but don't give me myself. But, this time, I feel whole and peaceful. I notice that those hours are like a gift. I haven't begun the day stressed out by all the things I have to do; I am just at one with myself. However, there's a limit to the silence I can endure, and, after half an hour, my mind fills with thoughts, such as, "What's the purpose of this silence?" and, "I still have so many things to do today," and, "It's a shame I'm wasting my precious time socarelessly."

I get up from the chair. My back hurts from the test and every movement must be calculated and much slower than usual. I sit at the computer and surf the Internet for a while but get fed up very quickly. I think about the things I have to do, trying to understand how the hell to fill myday.

For the last two days, I'd been running around preparing for the biopsy and my schedule was full. I had a clear purpose: to do everything that had to be done and repress my fears. The only things left to do now are the CT scans that'll take place in eight days, and to get some medical cover forms. What the hell am I supposed to do with all this free time?

As a patient, I always had somebody who managed my schedule, decided what tests I had to have, which treatment to go to, and I was busy all the time, trying to live and survive. It was my most important goal. Everybody around me (including the universe) rallied to help. I can't deny that there's something about it that's very convenient and releases you of all responsibility.

***

The unwritten commandments of the cancer patient:

1. **Take the word "cancer" in vain** – everywhere, at every opportunity, and in every way. Mention the word "cancer" to everyone you can who might be interested in hearing it. In return, you'll get great discounts, benefits and perks from *everyone*, without exception. Take full advantage of it. You never know when you'll have cancer again…

2. **Respect your nurses and doctors** – and treat them with tenderness, patience, and compassion. You're their responsibility for the time being. You don't want, God forbid, to anger them and thus make them spit in your chemotherapy or piss in your infusion.

3. **Take advantage of your friends and visitors as much as possible** – for rides, food, transportation, shopping, concerts, everything – at their expense! During this period, there's nothing they won't give you, the moment you ask. Don't hesitate to cross over to the dark side and request things that you usually wouldn't dare even think about. There's nothing like cancer to check boundaries and discover from whom you can extract anything and everything.

4. **Play on their conscience** – while you're sick. The period of your sickness is finite, so make the most of it. If you didn't already get what you wanted, don't be afraid to play on their conscience by mentioning cancer and

death. And don't feel guilty about playing on their conscience! If you survive, it'll be the only thing everyone will be interested in, and if you die, who cares what they think of you?

5. **Smoke medicinal marijuana** – whether you like getting high or not, whether you're pro- or anti-drugs, or if you're afraid of being a pothead! It's authorized in black and

white by the Ministry of Health. How many people can say that?

6. **Remain "ill" for a bit longer after your recovery** – because it's not easy to recover and get back to real life. Therefore, make the most of the "side effects" and your feelings of victimization for a few months until you return to your old self. Nobody checks your medical file. Look at it as a sort of honeymoon after the wedding.

7. **Make the most of your disabled parking permit** – if not for yourself, then in order to avoid the continuous nagging of your family and friends so they can park freely on pavements and in No Parking zones.

8. **You shall have no other cancer before me** – except, of course, there could be metastases.

If asked, I will after half an – of course – deny each of these clauses or say I have cancer.

REMISSION

Five days have passed since the biopsy, and I'm trying to think as little as possible about the results and the other tests. The back pains come and go, depending how much I deal with them. When I think that my back aches or that the results might not be good, it hurts much more. When I'm busy with my daily chores or routine activities, the pain is there, but minor.

No matter how much I try to fill my day with essential and meaningful things, I'm not reaching my full potential. A little voice in the background stops me, saying: "Buddy, think about it: it's entirely possible that this ritual of yours may change very soon, so don't hang on to it."

Every time such a thought surfaces, I try to accept it, and then try to replace it with thoughts of things that my friends or Orit have said. I think a lot about my grandmother and her attitude. I think about everything worth living for, things that make me happy. I think about my future goals and this motivates me and instills some life into me.

I decide to go on vacation to clear my head. I call Orit, tell her that I intend to travel spontaneously to the holiday destination of Eilat tomorrow morning, and ask if she's interested in joining me. She says yes, she'll gladly join me. I'm so happy that I won't be there by myself and especially that I'll be spending the next few days with her.

I call my good friend Ronen Haskel, director of the Nova-Like Hotel in Eilat, where I once worked as Entertainment Manager after the army, and I book a room.

I don't want anything unfamiliar now – not a new hotel, not some other girl, no new friends. I need firm ground, familiar, comfortable and loving. In any event, the rest of my life is unstable, to say the least, so the foundations need to be strong. I organize my bag excitedly, looking forward to some days of vacation and quiet.

Orit picks me up early in the morning and we're soon on our way to Eilat. The moment I see her, I'm full of joy. It warms my heart that she's with me. I can't stop blabbering and acting stupid. I'm anticipating the vacation ahead. But as the trip progresses, the same old thoughts start crowding my mind: why are we doing this to ourselves? What if I develop feelings for her? Why did I invite her on this trip if we don't know what's going to happen between us? We keep driving and there are moments of silence, which bother me a lot. Every second of silence adds another issue to the dilemma. Maybe she's not that into me, which is why she isn't talking? Maybe she regrets coming.

I'm an extreme person. It's hard for me to find the middle line, either this way or that.

She puts some music on, thus breaking the silence. I listen to the song's lyrics, which are in a language entirely foreign to me, and am swept away by it. The singer has a beautiful voice, one that penetrates my soul. The song cheers me up. I ask Orit who she is, and she tells me she's a musician she loves very much called Cesaria Evora, who hasn't had an easy life, to say the least. I feel as though I've known her for years. We keep listening to her songs one after the other, and I feel as though her voice shouts out my feelings and fears even though I can't understand a word that comes out of her mouth. I feel her in a profound way. All of a sudden, words seem superfluous.

I look at Orit, driving quietly, and I take her hand. She looks at me wordlessly. I feel her, and understand her, as though we have started a common language. The silence of her company seems less strange and threatening now.

We arrive in Eilat, drop our bags at the hotel, and go out. We enjoy every moment – eat in restaurants, go to the sea, to the swimming pool, shop, and live as though there's no tomorrow.

At a certain point, as we sit in a restaurant, I'm thoughtful. Orit immediately notices and asks what happened. I share with her my fears about the biopsy results and tell her I'm considering calling my oncologist to check if he has heard anything.

"What good will knowing the results do? What can it change right now? Enjoy yourself, you'll have enough time for that later," she says simply. It's liberating to know I can have a vacation like this one, and enjoy it without boundaries or obstacles. I feel my energy and strength return. I can even meditate every morning like I used to.

I remember, weird as it may sound, that the period of my sickness was one of the happiest in my life! I lived every day as though it was the last, despite the difficult experiences. So what's different now?

***

It's not easy to live, knowing that you may die at any given moment on any day. Even when you're healthy, you can die at any time. However, there's one essential difference: you can repress death, convince yourself that it won't happen to you, or believe and hope that, before your time comes, science will discover the medicine that'll keep you alive.

As a cancer patient, you don't have that privilege. Even if you want to repress death, it's there around you, lurking above you at any given moment, your partner for the road, and it would be a good thing for you to connect with him.

If you ask a healthy man what his plans are for the day, he'll answer, "Get up, eat, go to work, travel, see my wife in the evening."

When people used to ask me during my sickness what my plans were, I used to answer, "Get up! That's enough for now. Let me just get past this critical phase."

Everything you do during the day makes you forget death. The moment the thought pops into your mind, you can bury it with a dance, watch a good film, or have sex. If you don't have time to watch a movie or have sex, you can combine the two and watch a film with sex scenes. The repression mechanism is charged and ready to shoot at any given moment.

When I was sick, even when I succeeded in repressing that thought, doctors would immediately lean over and remind me that their white robes didn't mean it was a pamper evening in the spa.

When you live a normal life, you can console yourself by

going to a good restaurant or eating ice cream that contains so much sugar it could kill you faster than life itself.

When I was hospitalized, the only thing I could console myself with was hospital food and jello for dessert. I really don't know what's better – hospital food, or death.

Not that I don't appreciate the food. I do, really. Children in Africa may have nothing to eat, but I'm pretty sure that, given hospital food, they'd say, "No thank you, we'll go catch a zebra!"

People institutionalized in the hospital should be given pampering food. It's hard enough for them. And I mean in *all* institutes. For instance, it always amazes me when I see films where a prisoner goes on hunger strike, and every day one of the guards comes and puts prison food near his bed, hoping he'll be tempted to eat and thus break his strike. Every time I watch such a scene, I'm in shock. I mean, are you serious? The guy hasn't eaten for two and a half weeks… do they really think that mashed potatoes and last week's vegetables that look like someone vomited them onto the plate will tempt him? *This* is supposed to make him break all his principles? His plate just offers confirmation as to why it's worth dying. You want to pique his appetite? Offer him something delicious.

No court would convict a prisoner who continues his hunger strike because of disgusting food. Even the strictest judge has feelings.

In any case, I gotta run. I don't have a lot of time and I have to repress death.

BACK TO REALITY

It's midday, the third day of the vacation's about to end, and in another hour we'll be on our way home. I pack the bags and a deep sadness overwhelms me. Every item going in the bag symbolizes my return to the chaos that awaits me at home, and to reality. I make every effort to remember that I can have fun there, too – it's only a matter of choice – and yet, the thoughts running through my head continue to shatter my recent tranquility.

I understand that the trip to Eilat doesn't mean the situation I must face in the future has disappeared. This is something I can't run away from. I can't run away from myself; I go everywhere with myself.

I leave the bags, go to Orit, and start trying to make her laugh. I catch her, throw her in the air, try in every way to hold on to my previous energy, gain a few more moments of grace. She smiles at me and requests some time to herself to practice some yoga before we embark on our journey back.

I leave her, continue packing the bags, and look at her, breathing and patiently relating to space. The first thought that comes into my mind is, "Seriously, what *is* this nonsense? Have some fun! Isn't this a waste of time?" But the more I look at her, at her ease, the peace and quiet that she's currently experiencing, I envy her. I also want to be there. I'm frustrated with myself. Why can't I be like that? Why do I always have to be so frenetic? I keep looking at her, and I can't stop. She fascinates me, fills me, charges my soul. The more I look at her, the calmer I feel. My thoughts change and I'm grateful to have this amazing person to balance me. I'm glad I'm not like her and she's not like me, because otherwise we wouldn't have clicked in this special way.

But most of all, I'm grateful that, even though I don't often love myself and I'm not at peace with myself, I wouldn't change anything in myself, or anything that comes with it.

***

I can say for sure, without any hesitation, with no regrets and no reservations, that the period during which I had cancer was beneficial, and that I gained something that there was no chance I would ever experience again in a million years (assuming, with excessive optimism, that I'll live that long). I was relieved of an enormous burden, a suffocating feeling, a layer of difficulty that simply evaporated as though it had never existed. I'm talking about the fact that all the hair on my body fell out. I was never so smooth as I was during that period. Like a baby's ass.

It wasn't easy. The chemotherapy had to work very hard in my case because, even though it's so expert at spreading toxins and eliminating hair cells, and even though it has removed trillions of hairs during millions of treatments worldwide, and even though it has international certifications, it had to outdo itself to eliminate the amount of hair I had!

Before the treatment, my entire body, every inch of it, was covered with hair. My hands, my legs, my back, my shoulders, my stomach, my nose, everywhere. And I'm not talking about regular hair, but a pelt: King-Kong density and thickness, more concentrated than the rainforests of Brazil. The quantities were huge; I had the hair of eight people.

Just so you understand how hairy I was:

1. When I was born, the doctor told my mother, "Mrs. Eltawil, there are complications." She asked, "What do you mean? There are problems with the birth?" and they answered, "No. The baby's simply covered in tangles."

2. When I was born, the doctor told my mother, "Congratulations, you gave birth to a ball of fluff!"

3. I wasn't attached by my umbilical cord, but by the hair in my nose.
4. I went to a beautician who specialized in hair removal, and who guaranteed 100 percent success. After seeing me, the only thing she'd commit to was a 100 percent chance she *wouldn't* succeed.
5. I had to use a lawn mower on my chest.
6. I'd shave the right side of my face, and by the time I'd finished the left side, I was already sprouting a new beard on the right.
7. In a theater performance, I played a bush. The director told me I didn't need a costume.
8. When I'd come out of the shower, I didn't bother with a towel. I just got straight into the dryer.

When I was healthy, there were times when my hairiness was a real bummer. Sometimes, I'd look at myself and long for something else, to be someone else, to have another body. I'd look at hairless people on the beach and ask myself if, one day, I'd look like that. And then, it simply happened, unexpectedly.

The best thing was that I didn't have to deal with snide comments anymore, which, until then, were an integral part of my life, such as this one: "Dude, it's the middle of summer. Why are you wearing a sweater?"

On the contrary, I was the recipient of supportive and encouraging comments. For example, during my treatment, a girl told me, "You're really handsome. If I'd known you looked like this, I'd have made a pass at you long ago."

The comment of the year goes to an acquaintance of mine, who didn't know I was sick and whom I met on the street at the peak of my sickness. (This is what she said, word for word, I swear.)

She: "What's this? You look fantastic! Did you get laser hair removal?"

Me: "No, sweetie, I'm having treatment."

She: "No! You're so clever! What kind of treatment? I've been trying to remove my unwanted hair for years, and I never got such great results."

Me: "No… they're chemical treatments."

She: "No way! Gimme the phone number of that place! I have to make an appointment!"

Me: "Why don't you save the money and buy yourself a brain instead?" (This, I said to myself, but really felt like saying it to her).

It was amazing and different to finally be hairless. It's great to hear compliments and feel admired, courted, and sexy. I was the house model of the Israeli Cancer Association. But it wasn't really me. And if I need cancer or some other thing in order to have others approve of me, then – no thanks.

Today, I'm healthy *and* hairy. Yes, yes, the hair grew back. Not in the same quantity – it takes quite a few years to reach that level – but it grew back and is an integral part of me. The truth? Today, I love every hair on my body, and I even thank them for being a part of me.

Sometimes, when I see smooth men shirtless, I still wonder if I can ever be like that some day? But I don't really want it anymore. I've been there, and I'm happy as I am.

PLAYING SAFE

We travel back to Tel-Aviv. The entire way back, I think of calling the oncologist and asking him if he's received the biopsy results. I have a burning need to know the results, but I don't call, firstly because I want a few more minutes of grace, and, secondly because I don't want Orit to hear the conversation. I prefer her to remember the fun we had during our vacation. We arrive in Tel-Aviv and she drops me at home, the ultimate sign that the fun is over. I say goodbye and go upstairs. The first thing I do is call the oncologist. Every ring equals ten heartbeats. My heart beats so fast I'm sure I'll die before he answers.

Then, I hear him at the other end of the line. He logs into his computer, searching for the results and tells me they haven't arrived yet, and that it will probably take another few days. He reminds me that the appointment for the stomach, chest and pelvis CT is scheduled for the next day. I thank him, we end the conversation, and I try to return to my business.

I have so many things to do that I quickly forget I've been on vacation. I look at all the things I have to do, and it depresses me. I don't know where to begin. I have to pick up the CT medical cover form, I have about sixty e-mails to take care of, but the most important thing is that in just *four days* my show, The Cancer That Died of Laughter, goes on. I just can't deal with it, mentally or physically, and choose to repress it.

I go back to my e-mails, the source of my livelihood and financial security. Since I recovered from cancer, I've been busy stabilizing my life, returning to my routine, trying to understand what I went through during the sickness and its effect on me, on who I am, and who I want to be in this life. I don't want to do anything that didn't serve me well in the past or made me feel bad. I'm trying to do only the things I like to do, and not compromise. It's really hard because, when I was sick, I reached realizations and understood situations that are worth 100 years of life experience. As a result, it left my body and mind in a traumatic state, long after my treatment was over and I'd returned to my regular life.

I knew that only a stable job, with regular hours, would allow me the calm I needed to make the right choices. I also knew that it would be pretty hard, because I'm not a man who sticks to routine, and never was. I'm used to jumping from project to project. Process and routine unsettle me, and commitment frightens me. But I felt, deep down, that I needed this. It was another step toward maturity and rebuilding myself.

I found an office job as a project manager in charge of entertainment. I'm glad I made that choice. I'm much closer to myself than I was in the past. It was the anchor and foundation for my development, for my rebirth. All this growing up was made possible because, first and foremost, this place provided me with financial security.

During the last few days in Eilat, I lived like there was no tomorrow, had a good time, and spent money. But now real life's knocking on my door and I have to remember that I must support myself and provide some security in case I'm unable to work in the future. There are no promises that I'll have the luck I had when I was sick, or that I'll have such rare people around me.

***

Money isn't everything in life. Unless you don't have it. One of the most amazing things that I experienced during my sickness was the fundraising event organized by my family, my friends, and people I didn't even know until then, who'd turned out to be very decent. Maya Angelou said: "People will forget what you said, and what you did, but they'll never forget how you made them feel."

For those of you who've never been the beneficiary of a fundraiser event – and I hope from the bottom of my heart that you're never going to need one – let me explain it to you: it's exactly like a wedding. Lots of guests, lots of checks, a one-time event (though nothing's guaranteed with a wedding or in sickness), you're in the spotlight, all the focus is on you, everybody's there for you, fluttering around you and showering you with love every minute... it's *so* confusing. As we went in, a friend of mine, a bachelor, gave me a kiss and hugged me, and I said to him, "God willing, it'll be your turn soon...."

I even looked like a groom. My friends dressed me up in a new shirt from Zara, a hat from Castro, trousers from Dolce & Gabbana, and shoes by Gucci. I didn't look sick, I looked like a benefactor. At the reception, someone collecting money came up to me and said, "Can you donate 50 bucks for the sick guy we're holding this fundraising event for?"

It took place in a hall, too. Actually, it was the Comedy Club Entertainment Hall, not a wedding hall, but still a hall. My friends appeared in sketches and did standup routines, and even I did a standup on cancer.

And if that wasn't enough, my date was called Cancer.

It wasn't easy for me to be in this position. I find it very hard to feel needy, so when one of my friends proposed that we organize this fundraising event, I adamantly refused. One day, my good friend, Vered Feldman, visited me in hospital and asked, "Why are you so stubborn?"

I said to her, "It's hard for me to be in the position of a 'weak person' and accept help from others."

She looked me in the eyes and said, "Then maybe you should understand that this is something you must learn to accept and deal with?" and left the room. This sentence kept coming back to me for a long time until I finally agreed. This was one of the most important and essential decisions I made; apart from the fact it helped me survive, it helped me see that I shouldn't be afraid to ask for help from my friends.

The fundraiser was important because I needed that money in order to channel all my strength and energy into surviving. I didn't even know how much. The money allowed me to try alternative medicines and undergo alternative treatments, which also healed my soul, and to buy healthy food to balance all the toxins poured into my body. What's more, I had to undergo other tests and get extra medical opinions that weren't covered by the insurance.

At first, it felt strange, because it was the first time in my life that I had so much money. Until then, I only had pennies in my bank account, I was always in debt, and when I went to draw money from the ATM machine, it didn't print a receipt because there wasn't enough money to cover its cost. Now, I could do whatever I wanted without a care in the world. I could stroll into the Medicare Clinic like a sheik and say to the nurse, "Give me this medicine, those injections and that solution for nausea! How much is that? A hundred bucks? What a joke! Take two hundred, keep the change, and one more word from you and I'll buy that inhaler machine for two hundred and fifty bucks, so watch out." I was a king!

The proceeds from the event were high: 25,000 Shekels (about $7000) just in case someone from Income Tax is reading this; 50,000 Shekels (about $14000) for a regular reader. There were 400 people, and each paid a minimum of 100 Shekels (about $29) per ticket. It was worth being sick. There were also other donations besides the event, but don't worry, I spent everything on the sickness and on the Mercedes I bought to commute to my treatments. However, let's not dwell on this, I have to end this chapter because I have a flight to Thailand in another four hours.

So, today my Cancer spouse and I are divorced and I've no intention of going back to her – ever. I also have no intention of returning the checks I received.... This is what I'll do: I will always remember the people who organized the event and were with me during that period. Their big hearts and the event itself are the main reasons I'm alive today (and traveling to Thailand). I'll never forget how they made me feel.

NOTHING IS INSURED

Work helps me focus on matters at hand. Eilat becomes a vague memory even though it happened just a short time ago. Being busy gives me the structure I need and I hold on to it. This helps distract me from the thoughts of the test I have to go through tomorrow. I'm so busy sending emails, talking to clients, closing deals with entertainers… yet, despite the security and stability I feel from having a regular job in life, I'm also well aware of the fact that, if the results say that the cancer has recurred, I may not be able to hold on to this job or even worse, to operate or function. All the security I have right now may collapse like a deck of cards, and what then? The thought immediately makes me feel unstable. I start adding up all the money I spent in Eilat to pay back my soul for this period, and it adds up to a large sum. I'm not frugal, and I try to live every day as pleasantly as possible, as though it were my last day. But this time I feel some regret and I can't shake off this feeling. I'm mad at myself for this extravagance and keep thinking, *You're irresponsible! You don't think ahead! Wouldn't it have been more sensible to save this money in case you needed it in the future to save your life? What'll happen if you need more money for treatment? Or for survival?* Even though I've witnessed that, in critical moments in life, there are always good people to support and take care of me, I don't see myself going through another fundraising event and asking people to help me. What if there are tests to pay out of my own pocket? How will I pay them? I've no property of my own, nor any savings. I've never thought that far ahead. What collateral do I have that will help me should the cancer recur, God forbid?

***

Every day I thank God, the universe, and everyone possible, but above all my mother, who was smart enough to purchase private medical insurance for me at a time when I was stupid. Undoubtedly, it's the most sensible thing she's ever done for me (besides the amazing feat of bringing such a special, sexy guy as me into this world). The insurance helped me to stay alive and ask the question: "How the hell would I have survived without it?" Thanks to it, I was able to obtain second opinions, further tests, and even send my tumor abroad.

Something about insurance gives you a false feeling of security. In difficult times, there's someone who'll look after you, save you when all else seems lost. My entire life, I looked for someone who'd give me an answer, promise me everything would be all right, give me security and assure me that everything could be alright in life. Insurance gives you an answer. To sum up: **We're all looking for security in life and there's nothing like insurance to convince you that there's no insurance against anything.**

Officially, and without question, I am the biggest nightmare, the greatest anxiety, the "monster" that every private insurance company prays they will never have knock on their door: a serial patient. Here are a few minor examples of what I've been through during my life.

1. At the age of twenty, I had a motorcycle accident. I broke some bones in my back and my chest, and smashed my hand (don't worry, it wasn't my strong right hand, the one with which... never mind), and if that wasn't enough, I also smashed my spleen.

2. At the age of twenty-five, I was diagnosed with a tumor in my thigh.

3. At the age of twenty-seven, playing football, I tore a knee ligament and underwent surgery to have it reconstructed. (For those of you who are wondering, this terminated my promising career as a soccer player. Leo Messi, you can breathe easy now.)

4. At the age of thirty-one, I was diagnosed with cancer. (I know this surprises you the most.)

5. As part of the cancer treatment, I underwent two operations to remove the tumors, during which, just to play it safe, the doctors also removed a number of organs, which, in themselves, would have been enough to construct another human being.

I had a few more little incidents in my life, which I'm not sure whether to mention or not, such as:

–At the age of three, I lost a tooth (and even though I put it under my pillow, to this day I still haven't received the flying dinosaur I was promised).
–At the age of eight, I banged my nose against the wall and was taken to the hospital. That incident ended with a few stitches. Considering the size of my nose, the wall wasn't as lucky and collapsed. May it rest in peace.

In short, there isn't a part of my body that isn't damaged. I know the human body perfectly: I am a kind of specialist. I am every over-achieving mother's dream, only without ever having studied medicine. I can give advice on medical matters. Sometimes the HMO refers patients to me for advice.

I'm sure there must be a big photo of me hanging on the office walls of the insurance companies in Israel, next to this sign: Do not ever, under any circumstances, contact this man! Insurance company trainees are taught how to never repeat the mistake called "Eyal Eltawil" with other clients. They no longer answer my calls; if I want to reach them, I call from an unidentified number.

When you come to think of it, it's understandable. The insurance company's aim is to make money, and sick people don't help them achieve this goal. When they want to sell you a policy, they'll stoop to any means to get your money: they'll tell you that you can be wounded, that you can die (as though if I buy a policy, I won't die sometime, anyway), that you'll grow old, and are bound to suffer until the end of your life unless you purchase all their policies: medical, geriatric care, extra A, B and C, bullshit insurance, pre-bullshit insurance, insurance for bullshit insurance... and even so, you'll most probably get to the bullshit phase, including a large debt to the bank.

But if, God forbid, you want to use their services and hope to solve your problems and, in the process, you actually make them lose money, it will definitely not suit their concept.

They'll find every way possible to prevent you from getting the money or, if they have no choice, give you only part of it. They'll also find a nice, suitable name for it – personal participation... that sounds much more pleasant than its true definition: screwing you.

It's absurd to have to pay money for insurance, and even more absurd that when something does happen to you, you have to share the money you already paid. And if I never get hurt and never have to use insurance money, am I not supposed to receive "personal participation" for all the money I paid them?

But the most important thing is to buy an insurance policy while you're still healthy!

I, for example, wanted to buy life insurance after I recovered from cancer, but was flatly refused, claiming that (this sentence was said to me, word for word, on the phone. I changed nothing): "Due to what you have been through lately, we cannot insure you. We are sorry, but we only insure healthy people. Try us again in five years' time, when you've distanced yourself from the sickness." *What*? Doesn't that somehow contradict your concept?

The insurance company will never insure you after you get sick or injured because you're worth their time only when you're healthy. They'll find any way possible to prevent you from activating the policy; they'll also thoroughly investigate every detail of your medical history, anything that will provide them with the perfect excuse not to insure you.

Them: "Excuse me, what's *that*?"
You: "A scratch on my leg."
Them: "Due to surgery you had in the past?"
You: "No, not at all. I got a scratch from a bush."
Them: "We understand… did the bush undergo surgery in the past?"
You: "*What*? How should I know?"

Them: "Is this bush a direct relative of yours?"
You: "No, it's just a bush I brushed by on the street!"
Them: "Okay. We just have to check if the bush's family has a history of scratches and we'll get back to you in about two years."

Insurance companies regard a sick person like he's a car with a damaged chassis, whose value has decreased, and it's not worth investing in him. He's not worth the trouble. As far as they're concerned, you can go sell yourself for scrap.

These are the things you usually think about when something happens (unless you have my mother, but that doesn't make sense, because I'm not aware of any more brothers).

When I was young, I never thought about life insurance, because when you're young, you're not afraid of death, you're too busy conquering the world, denying the future, acting foolishly, making mischief, enjoying life, and you're sure nothing bad will ever happen to you and that you'll live forever. Well, I declare, here and now, that it's not true, because if Christopher "Superman" Reeve – our childhood hero who, in our eyes, could conquer everything – ended his life as a paraplegic in real life, then it can happen. (It's true! Google him!) He was *Superman*! He saved the world, hovered between continents, fought all the bad people and won effortlessly. Then he got on a horse, fell off, broke his spine, and became paralyzed. If even he needed insurance, then we all do.

Private insurance isn't cheap and not everyone can afford it. **Private insurance is so expensive that it's not worth being healthy.** It's worth catching some disease in order to cover the investment.

After a CT scan, the doctor said to me, "I'm pleased to say your tests are fine!"

"Are you sure?" I asked. "Let's check again, maybe during the next scan the radiation will do some damage."

You take out insurance policies to feel safe, but the only sure thing about insurance is that it will leave you broke.

TARGET PRACTICE

Morning dawns and I go to the hospital for my tests. Since my recovery, I've had a CT scan every few months to make sure the cancer hasn't recurred. Up to now, the tests have always been clean. That doesn't mean that I'm not profoundly anxious before each test, or that I'm not nervous and full of "what-ifs." I generally had no real reason for concern, though, which made it less critical and hysterical for me. This time it's different. There's a specific reason for this test.

I reach the ward, present the forms, sit down, and wait my turn. Usually the wait for a CT scan is long because the waiting room's full of people. This time, the place is nearly empty, as though there are no more diseases and everybody is healthy. The only person waiting is a woman sitting at the end of the corridor. I look at her; she's watching the news on TV. The news anchor reports a serious accident, gravely overstating the horrible event, explaining that, even though the state of the passengers is yet unknown, no one could survive such a terrible wreckage. Every word is like a knife in the viewer's heart, and the woman can't take her eyes off the screen, captivated by the story.

I try to imagine the drama currently going on in her life. Why is she here? Does she really need to watch these catastrophes on TV? Or maybe she prefers the problems of others rather than her own? The doctor calls her and she doesn't even notice. I turn to her and ask her if it's her name that has just been called and she says yes, leaves the TV, and enters her own private drama.

I turn off the TV and remain sitting. A few moments later, my turn comes. I go in, say hello to the medical team, who know me from the dozens of previous times I've been here. I'm a VIP of the CT ward. I lie down inside the machine and the technician starts the scan. I'm inside a round space that glides forwards and backwards, making endless sounds, while I'm stuck, silent, unable to move, staring at the machine's ceiling. The technician tells me from time to time to hold my breath for the test. If only he knew how many times I stop breathing, even when he doesn't tell me to. I feel like I'm suffocating, pressed and trapped. The only thing that doesn't stop moving are my thoughts. They broadcast to me aggressively that I don't want to be there, that maybe I shouldn't be there. All of a sudden, I don't care that this test could later save me. All I can think of is, "What the hell am I doing here now?"

Three months ago, everything was clean, so isn't it a shame that I'm pouring all this poison into my body even before the results of the biopsy are known?

From the moment I knew there was a possibility the cancer had recurred, I've been running around constantly, without stopping for a moment to think what I was doing, and the consequences. Am I doing the right thing? I'm just accepting the situation like a robot.

***

When I was sick, I underwent a lot of treatment, from chemotherapy to a bone marrow transplant, all of them with a common goal: to save me. It was done very clearly. Into my body, the medical team poured sufficient toxins to wipe Iraq off the map. They hoped it would kill the cancer or at least allow me to live long enough to conduct negotiations with it.

My general state and the instantaneous and future implications of the treatment were of no importance during this period. The main goal was to "gain time," which, by the way, could be several days, months, and sometimes years, because, as it turns out, it's better to destroy you over a period of time than all at once.

However, there is one radically different treatment, and not a pleasant one at that. Although the treatment doesn't contain rosewater or fairy dust, at least they try to treat the specific area of the cancer. And by that, I mean radiology.

Before the treatment, I faced a serious dilemma. This was the last treatment in the protocol and my entire body was clean; no tumor was visible on the horizon. I was in great shape and the treatment had been very effective. I debated with myself on the question: if everything bad had been eliminated by the previous treatment, why did I need another specific one now?

On the one hand, I could have refused the treatment, even though the doctors recommended it and it was included in my protocol of treatment, thus reducing my chances of a long-term recovery, or, worse, risk hearing my doctors say, "We told you so."

On the other hand – in the short term, I had to take great care of my body, which had already endured so much damage from the chemo toxins and treatment. I didn't want to pour any more "treats" into it unless it was absolutely necessary. Of course, I didn't have an unequivocal answer regarding what was right or wrong. It was a difficult dilemma like other dilemmas in life, except that, this time, my life was at stake.

During the treatment, they direct the laser toward the problematic spot and try to eliminate it. They blast enormous quantities of radiation where the laser is focused, making you useful as a potential antennae for cell phone reception. At the peak of the radiation procedure, they made that very clear to me when I felt sick and was hospitalized in the emergency ward. After a few hours, one of the patients hospitalized with me had to have an X-ray and they requested everybody present, patients and visitors, to leave the room in case. God forbid that they should absorb some radiation! As I made to leave, the doctor looked at my medical file, which was on the bed, and said to me, "Forget, it, you can stay." What he meant was, "I asked them to leave the room in order to save them from exposure to radiation, and you, with the amount you have in your body, you want to kill them in the corridor?"

In another moment, he'd have removed the X-ray machine as well and given the patient an X-ray using my body. Good thing he covered my intimate parts in order to cover his conscience.

Radiology also has many advantages. For example, I don't need a microwave oven any more. The food enters my body raw and is cooked inside.

I was exhausted. It was the end of the treatment, and the end is always the most difficult. I didn't have the strength for treatment that seemed unnecessary. For six weeks I was supposed to report daily for radiation, go home, and come back the next day. All that went with it didn't encourage me much, either. Radiology is done inside machines with very "calming" names that give you a feeling of peace and quiet. My machine, for example, was called Accelerator 5, a gentle and quiet name, which made me think every second of the treatment would accelerate my demise. Accelerator 5 is a name better suited for a spacecraft or an atomic bomb. I'd have felt better if my machine had a nicer, lighter name. How about "Beautiful 21-Year-Old Swedish Girl Hopelessly in Love With Me."

And if that wasn't bad enough, my radiology treatments were scheduled for 07:30 in the morning – *every morning*! Excuse me? Do I look like a farmer? Even the accelerator doesn't wake up that early! For a moment, I thought I heard it shout, "Dammit, give me time to brush my teeth and get a coffee and come back in half an hour."

I'd have turned a blind eye at the name (Accelerator 5!), if at least the medical team had been assuring. During one of the radiation sessions, the doctor told me the X-ray showed that I had one kidney higher than the other. Apparently, one of my kidneys had decided to wear a stiletto…. I got a bit stressed and asked her, "What does *that* mean?" to which she answered: "Nothing to worry about, it's nothing, it's like someone who has one brown eye and one green eye."

Well, that reassured me like a guided missile aimed

at my head. Perhaps this was a nice comparison, but it wasn't very accurate, because if this non-existent person's brown eye was located higher than his green eye, say, on his forehead, it would have made him see things a bit differently….

In the end, I decided to undergo radiation. At least I can console myself that, generally speaking, I could have died, but, in fact, I am still alive.

IMPROVING EXPERIENCE

Since the test was done in the same clinic where I had the biopsy, when I'm done with the CT, I look for the doctor and nurse that did it in order to say hello. Only the nurse is there, but we talk and laugh. It's amazing how the mere sight of her makes me feel good and dissolves my anxiety. I tell her that the results haven't arrived yet and remind her of my show The Cancer That Died of Laughter, which will be on in three days. She tells me she'll be coming with her daughter, and the doctor will be coming with his wife. I'm really glad they'll be present and tell her I'll leave four tickets in her name.

I go out to the hospital lawn. I sit on the grass and examine the place, trying to take in every little detail. I look at the patients sitting and breathing the fresh air before returning to their hospital rooms. I look at the families accompanying them with so much love and care, at the doctors who experience this lovely open space amid their endless running from one ward to the other. I think about the vast difference between the bright green grass that surrounds me and the people stuck inside the buildings, who see only gray.

I lie on the grass and look at the sky, a huge, bright, blue space, an incomprehensible magic spread before and above me, and I feel helpless.

I survey the building where the oncology ward is located. I recognize it quickly and accurately, especially the room in which I was hospitalized for such a long time. I feel myself tense when I remember my time in that room and I want to get up and run, but something more powerful binds me to the ground and forces me to stay. I stare at the window of my room, trying to understand the feelings running through me when I remember that particular period. It's hard. I struggle not to get up and run and let myself feel. I lie there for about half an hour and think about the entire period, every doctor, every big test I underwent, and every small needle that penetrated my veins, and every bit of news I was given concerning my state. I allow myself to remember things that frighten me, and I start crying. Now, more than ever, I want to get up and run, but I feel that I have to cope with my fears, that this is a good time to get rid of the trauma, in case I have to return to the hospital. When I look it in the eye, it's frightening, but liberating, and the monster isn't as big.

When I get up from the grass, I feel dizzy, but the moment it passes, I feel enormously relieved. I decide to go back to the hospital and I'm lighter now. I wander around and visit every ward in which I had been hospitalized. I try to breathe, experience, and absorb the feeling.

Until now, I had only ever returned for routine tests. I did everything like a horse wearing blinkers; the only important thing was the goal, so nothing else was of interest to me.

I keep visiting the wards, saying hello to the doctors who took care of me, peek into the café, one of my "retreats" in the evenings, between one treatment and the other, where I went to drink orange juice. I can still taste the juice in my mouth.

I stop in front of one of the buildings and look at it. After a few seconds, I start laughing uncontrollably, a good and liberating laugh that comes from the heart. I'm pretty sure passersby looking at me must have said to themselves, "If that guy's looking for the mental health building, it's a little further along." But I can't stop. I don't care if anyone's looking at me or not. I don't give a damn what they think. I feel as sane as I've ever felt lately.

The building in front of me is the Male Fertility building, where I froze my sperm when I got sick, in order to ensure my chances of having children in the future.

What makes me laugh, apart from remembering everything I went through while freezing the sperm, is that it suddenly makes me realize the gap between how I'm sure my life should be, and what it actually is. Or, as John Lennon once said in one of his songs, "Life is what happens to you while you're busy making other plans."

***

I am a man, and as such, I hereby declare, that the word masturbation can't make me feel anything other than utter happiness and is generally followed by a deep sleep with a smile on my face! However, when it happens with regard to freezing sperm before chemotherapy starts, it's something else. And that's exactly what I had to do to ensure my future dynasty after the oncologist advised me that my sperm cells were about to die.

Before continuing, I would like to make something clear. My sperm is **dead forever, deceased. No way will it come**

back to life. It is completely destroyed! I apologize for being firm on the matter, it's simply that since I recovered, a few times – about a million – women have come up to me and asked: "What do you mean, you can't have children? You have no sperm at all?"

I explain that I have sperm, but the cells are dead.

She insists, and asks: "But when you come, do you have sperm"?

I keep explaining patiently that I have it, but that it's not functional.

Of course, she's not convinced and says to me, "Okay, if you have sperm, then use it!"

Oh, come on lady, what do you mean, use it?! What do you want me to do, bake a cake with it? Shall I wash my car with it? It's dead, may it rest in peace.

I know it may seem as though I'm a bit angry, and the truth is that I am. Freezing my sperm was a shock for me. I felt like a worthless man. The thought of going into a room where there were porn films and magazines and to use my hand to masturbate didn't seem in any way bad. I really believed so. As far as I was concerned, I thought it'd be an experience that was worth getting sick for. I'm a man!

When I called the Sperm Clinic and the nurse told me on the phone: "Come on, I'll show you how it works," I nearly burst out laughing. You? You want to explain to *me*? I've been doing this since the age of 11! I could give courses on the subject, if you want… there's a method in my name, the Eltawil Method, the one with a turnover: people masturbate all over the world and I get commission. I wouldn't be surprised if your husband owes me quite a large sum.

I really thought it would be easy, fun, a great experience. But it seems there's a big difference between masturbating for pleasure and masturbating in a public place.

First of all, it's a very bizarre situation. I woke up at 7:00 in the morning, put on jeans, a nice shirt, after shave, deodorant, left the house, said hello to all the neighbors, smiled at them and they smiled back, all the while thinking that I'm a normal guy living a regular life, without them having even an inkling that I'm on my way to an 8:00 appointment in order to masturbate.

I was a working man up to that moment. It didn't mean that I didn't masturbate at 8:00 in the morning – on the contrary, why not? but never with such a clear agenda and aim.

I passed many cars on the way whose drivers had no idea where I was going. Maybe they, too, might have been on the way to the Sperm Bank and I had no idea they were going there.

I reached the Sperm Bank, or to be more precise I reached the hospital it was in. I didn't know where the Sperm Bank was situated and that was a big mistake. It's not an everyday question. I got mixed up and became stressed, afraid I might miss my appointment. Finally, I turned to a young woman passing by and simply asked her, "Excuse me, do you know where I donate sperm here?"

From the look she gave me, I'm sure there's now an identikit image of myself hanging in the nearest police station. After embarrassing myself two or three more times, I turned to someone who gave me such a definite and enthusiastic answer that I was sure he came there every day just for fun.

I finally reached my destination: the Sperm Bank. Or, judging by the looks of those waiting there, a better description would be The Crime Bank.

I sat on the bench. Around me sat a few humiliated, tormented-looking men, like they were on the defendants' bench in court. It was amazing to see a group of men whose hobby is to masturbate in their free time look so impotent.

I felt humiliated, and just wanted my turn to come so that I could get out of that place. The trouble was that, here, one must wait his turn. There's no other option. It's not like a bank. You can't go over to someone and say: "Excuse me, I'm in a real hurry, do you mind if I masturbate before you? Just a little rub and I'm out. Thanks, that's very nice of you."

After five masturbators – who took their time – my turn came. While I was waiting, I got really angry at them. I thought to myself: *Hello! There are other masturbators outside, people who have to go to work!* But when I myself entered, I identified with them, I understood them. I myself was faced with the hard dilemma: on the one hand, there are people in the room outside waiting for their turn; and on the other hand, how many times in my life will I have the opportunity to masturbate in such a room without anyone bothering me, and with the doctor's approval, at that? Who knows when I'll have cancer again and be able to enjoy such a luxury?

I convinced myself that it had to do with my future child, and that I had to invest time in him, and that I didn't want him to be born after masturbating for just a minute and a half.

The sight was amazing. A spacious room, porn magazines, a selection of pornographic DVDs... I felt as though I was in the Himalayas. What views! And no passport needed.

I took my time, which was four minutes at the most. I finished and was already planning to leave, but then discovered how practiced I was at masturbation when I instinctively started to suppress evidence. I returned the magazines to their right places, changed the paper on the chair, removed the DVD and put it back on the shelf... like someone would enter after me and say to himself, "It's really clean and neat here, that other guy probably just read a book."

When I went outside, someone was already waiting his turn, and what amazed me was that a woman entered the room with him. I swear to you, I was in shock! It turned out that it was acceptable to bring help! I don't understand why a man would choose to bring a sandwich with him to a restaurant, but so be it…

I went to the clerk, holding the bottle in my hand. She was so professional and concentrated in her purpose that she let nothing distract her.

It's so important for a woman to work in this place, and not a man, because a woman understands the real and o-n-l-y importance of the sperm: to bring children into the world. For a woman, it is something holy. We men merely waste it indiscriminately.

By the way, I've no doubt that it was a woman who invented the Sperm Bank. It's so clear. When you come to freeze sperm, you're not allowed to masturbate for 48 hours before that, so that the sperm is strong. This is a law that only a woman can pass. A man would never say such a thing to another man, because he knows how difficult that is. If a man had been the one to establish the Sperm Bank, he would have developed a method where it would have been allowed to masturbate every ten minutes. The problem is that we don't have the time to develop such a method, because we are constantly busy masturbating.

I entrusted my sperm to the nice lady in the laboratory and went home, tired and happy, to get busy with my other things. It's a pity to waste life masturbating. Despite the relative trauma I experienced, I'll never stop masturbating; what's more, it might even happen today.

REBORN

Fifteen days have elapsed since the moment I was told that there was a chance the cancer had recurred, thirteen days since the biopsy and three days since the CT scan. Not a long time in day to day terms. An eternity in terms of how I feel and what I experience.

I'm waiting in suspense for the results, but something else bothers me more, and that's my performance in The Cancer That Died of Laughter, which will take place this evening.

I still have a few hours till the performance, and up to now, I've succeeded in repressing and dealing with it. The show's a sellout, the hall's fully booked, people are looking forward to hearing what I have to say. My public is waiting for me.

And it doesn't mean that I don't like to perform – I'm crazy about it. It fills me up. There's nothing better than seeing people laugh and enjoying themselves. It's worth everything in life.

But this time there are two key issues:

The first is that I feel like a hypocrite, a fake and a liar. I'm supposed to go on stage nonchalantly to make everybody laugh, while deep down I'm scared stiff and don't believe one word that comes out of my own mouth.

What right do I have to go on stage? I'm trying to show people that there's another way of dealing with things, to influence people's thinking regarding this disease and about any crisis in life. In the show, I talk about how much one can learn from a time like this, and benefit from it, and that we can laugh even about cancer. But I, a cancer superhero, am unable to listen to my own advice. I'm crashing, crying, suffering from anxiety. What does that make me as a person? What does that mean for the show!? I have to be funny!

Which leads me to the second issue: I don't *want* to be funny tonight. I don't feel as though I'm capable of laughing. All of a sudden, the show doesn't seem funny at all.

What the hell am I supposed to be laughing about here? There's a chance I'll soon be back where I started. I'm seriously thinking of cancelling the show, looking for excuses and logical explanations to justify this, but can't find any. What will I tell my public? That the only thing I want right now is to enter a time machine, my destination being the day after I get the results?

I know it's a lost cause. The show must go on. I pick up the scripts and try to memorize them as well as the jokes, but nothing sinks in.

Maybe I should call the oncologist and ask him if the results have arrived? If they're okay, I'll know I'm healthy and perform without telling the public lies. It would solve my problem. But the thought that the results may not be good stresses me too much.

I try to take my regular nap, but am unable to do so. I get out of bed and go for a walk, breathe some air. I still have three hours before I have to go. I see all the people walking about, laughing, enjoying themselves, feeling free… I, too, want that so much, but without success. I feel like screaming at them, "Why are you so happy??!! Everything's temporary! There's a chance I'll die soon!"

I return home sooner than planned, organize all my stuff and go on my way. I reach the hall and put everything in its place, just like for every regular show. Nobody around me knows what I'm going through. I, myself, hardly know what I'm going through.

I go to the dressing room and try to relax while the hall fills up. Usually, everyone coming in and all the noise adds to the excitement before the start of the show and fills me with enthusiasm. Now, every person entering the hall raises my blood pressure and increases my level of anxiety. I peep at them around the door, praying they'll change their minds and go home. But they come in one by one, smiling, laughing as though there was no tomorrow. *What the hell are they laughing at?!* I think to myself.

The usher comes over to me enthusiastically and informs me that the audience is nearly in, that the hall's entirely full, and that we'll be starting in a few minutes.

And that's when it happens. The announcer presents me and my show. I put on the intro video and, as soon as it ends, I go on.

I stand opposite the public, a big smile on my face, feeling as hypocritical as ever, scared they'll call my bluff. I try to breathe, try to keep the smile on my face for as long as possible, try to convince myself. I look at them one by one as I do in every show, except that this time they seem to me much bigger, scarier and more threatening. I register in the corner the doctor and the nurse I invited, and I'm filled with fright that I might let them down after all they did for me. I introduce myself and deliver the lines with which I open every performance: "I've been clean and healthy for over three years. I recovered entirely from cancer."

The thought that it might not be true takes hold of me, but then the public starts clapping and I go on to my first joke, after which everybody laughs. It relieves me a little. I continue with the show… it's getting good, and the audience is laughing, listening, getting excited. But something more amazing happens to me: this is the first time that I myself listen to the performance, and I find that every sentence carries huge significance. I'm performing for myself, too. My words make me remember all that I believe in with all my heart.

All of a sudden, I don't care if the cancer recurs or not, or if the public knows what state I'm in. It's irrelevant. What *is* relevant is the here and now, the fact that they're enjoying *now*, the fact that I'm enjoying *now*, the fact that the truth of what I want to say is much bigger than anything tomorrow will bring. The *now* will remain forever, after I and others have passed away.

I am living the moment. Only the here and now is relevant to me, without thinking about what will happen in the end, or about the end. I continue with the performance and I feel relieved, alive, real, and genuine. I succeed in believing in myself.

I see the doctor and the nurse hooting with laughter, and I know that the fact that they came here today is the greatest triumph of all, and no result I may receive can change that.

The performance ends and everybody applauds. I look

at them, but in fact, I'm looking at myself, because the fact that they didn't judge me allows me not to judge myself, and to follow my belief.

I smile and thank them from the bottom of my heart for the lesson I've learned because of them, on how lucky I am to be with them at the moment, for the gift of being alive. I thank God. Never mind what the results bring – I thank him for being alive.

***

Birthdays are celebrated once a year. They commemorate the special day on which you were born, in which you came into the world, in which your special personality, that has no other like it, entered the space of the universe with the aim of influencing it in your unique way.

Cancer made it possible for me to remember, every moment, how much fun it is to have come into this world and that it's in no way obvious.

On a day-to-day basis, on the endless chase for significance, it's easy to forget that. Many people whine about their bitter fate and don't celebrate that date, thinking: "It's just a birthday, why make such a fuss?" or, "I'm already old, what reason do I have to celebrate?"

Ever since I recovered, I've celebrated my birthday according to a new recount. I threw a big party for "my new birth," then a birthday at the age of one, two, and three, and I'm looking forward to many more birthdays. Celebrating a birthday as a cancer patient is different than a regular birthday, for many reasons:

1. When your friends sing the Israeli birthday song and come to the line: "May you live till next year," you hope deep down that they're right, and that they understand the deep meaning of what they're saying. When they come to the line, "May you reach 120" and sing it with enthusiasm, you understand that they've absolutely no idea, that they're too optimistic, or that they're simply high on the drugs you procured for them.

2. You're spared the trouble of returning presents you don't like to the shop. Usually, there are no receipts with the presents you're given, because no one knows if you'll live long enough to return them.

3. A birthday spent in hospital is highly economical! You can't light candles on the cake because there are smoke detectors in every corner of the room. There's no need for a cake, anyway, because you'll probably throw up half a minute after eating a piece, due to the side effects of the chemotherapy.

4. In Israel, we say that when an eyelash falls out, you get a wish, so you won't need candles on your birthday cake to get a wish – you'll have thousands of them, because all your eyelashes will have fallen out!

5. It's an Israeli tradition that, on your birthday, your friends and family lift you up on a chair. You needn't feel bad about people many times your age lifting you up (then staggering away, panting, as though they've just run a marathon…). You hardly weigh 20 kgs! The cake they brought weighs more than you.

When people bless you, they make sure to wish you all the kinds of wishes available, so that in case you don't get to fulfil them, at least you'll have heard them before passing into the next world. But the truth is that it really doesn't matter, because the most important wish is: "Good health!"

THE TRUTH LIBERATES

A day after the performance, the adrenaline's still flowing and charging my body, making me feel alive. The excitement of what I experienced the day before doesn't leave me. I feel like I have a new life, that I've been reborn. Only one thing still puts a damper on my mood: the results of my tests, still unknown to me.

This time I don't hesitate. I pick up the phone and call the oncologist, knowing that no matter what happens, even if – God forbid – the results aren't good, I'll continue writing, performing, and creating. And even if I have to start treatment again, and even if I know my life will end soon, at least I'll be sure that I've lived every moment with my deepest truth.

I suddenly realize that there's no such thing as "I was sick, but now I'm healthy." It doesn't mean that it's ended and that I have gone on with my life and nothing will ever happen to me again.

I remember that the period of the sickness as a time when I felt healthier than any other time in my life. I lived every moment as though it was my last day. I can't disconnect and just unplug the cancer because, at the end of the day, I have no future without the past.

If it wasn't for that period, this book would never have

been written. There would have been no performance or other projects, I wouldn't have learned so many things about life, and I wouldn't have understood how amazing people are and how it's worth living just for them.

My doctor answers the phone, we talk for a few seconds and then he logs on to his computer to check the results, and informs me that he's got the result of the biopsy, but not of the CT. I can hear in his voice how important it is for him that the news is good, feel his alertness, which reminds me again how much I love and appreciate him. I wait. The silence between every word that comes out of his mouth makes me feel threatened.

And then he says to me: "Well, I'm sorry to disappoint…" I stop breathing, I don't believe I'm hearing this, but I'm ready for the worst, however bad it is. And then he continues: "but in the meantime, you're not about to die. Your tests are good." I let out a sigh of relief. We laugh together. The laughter changes to crying and I don't really care that he hears me, don't care if everybody knows I'm crying – it relieves so much tension and stress.

The minute our conversation ends, I call Orit. There's no one I want to talk to now more than her. I tell her the wonderful news, and she says she's so happy and content and that she knew from the first moment that this is how it would be. I listen to her, to every word that comes out of her mouth, her words of wisdom, and I'm happy that she's in my life, so happy that we didn't break up despite my initial reservations. I love her and I want her by my side always, until the happy end.

***

Three days later, I call the oncologist and hear from him that the CT scans were entirely clean and that there's no sign of the cancer recurring.

I'm so happy to hear that I'm healthy, but most of all I'm grateful for everything I've learned during this period.

ACKNOWLEDGEMENTS

I would like to say a huge thank you to a few people who, without them, I had no right to exist, and had it not been for them this book would never have been published.

- To my wonderful, dedicated, and special mother, who translated this book with a lot of love and passion. You are the number-one mother in the world.
- To my amazing family, my mother Miriam, my dad Benny, my sister Meital, and my brother Erez. Just for you, every moment is worth living. I love you from the bottom of my heart.
- To Orit Dembsky, my partner and the love of my life, for your support and help while I was writing this book, and of course for being with me every moment during the difficult period I went through when I really feared the cancer had recurred. Thanks to you, I knew I was in the 20% and that I would overcome. You, who made sure to clarify that you would always be there, whatever the situation, and taught me what true love is. (By the way, today she's my wife.)
- To my nephews, Bar and Itai – just by looking at you I'm filled with life and strength to move on.
- To all my uncles, aunts and cousins, to my brother-in-law

and to all those who were beside me during that period: there's no one like you! True, one does not choose one's family, but I got a good deal.

- To all my friends who were with me during that period, and are still in my life, and whom I won't name one by one, because there were so many that I really don't want to forget even one of you wonderful persons. Thank you all! Each of you is the greatest present I could ever have requested in life.
- To my literary editor, Noa Bareket, for the inspiration, the amazing editing, the accuracy, the ideas, and for letting me be myself in the most personal way, while knowing I had someone I could count on.
- To my English editors, Amit and Julie: thank you for your effort, your guidance and your uncompromising professionalism, and the heart and soul you poured into this project.
- To my illustrator, Hila Dabi: every word on your endless talent is superfluous. I couldn't have asked for someone who would understand in a better way what I wanted to express through the illustrations.
- To the team of dedicated employees of Focus Publications: Ronit Michlis, Tamy Trecht and Inbal Valencia, and to its director, Dr. Shaul Tal, on your warmth, humanity, and patience.
- To all those who supported the Headstart project: without you, this book would never have been published. Thank you for your belief in me and for your kind and generous support.

- To the doctors, the surgeons, the nurses and all the dedicated team of the Beilinson Hospital, for taking care of me during the entire period of my sickness and doing everything to make me feel good and recover. I guess that, as a dead man, it would have been hard for me to feel and write this book.

- To the amazing Professor Kashtan, for being there for me from the first moment the cancer was diagnosed and having remained in my heart since.

- To all the alternative care practitioners in the Beilinson Hospital Department of Alternative Medicine, whose dedication healed my soul, to Sharon Bar-Gil, whose nutrition and recipes supported my body, to Orly Tamir, for the acupuncture that eased the pain and the soul, to the devoted Dr. Ofer Caspi, the director of the department, to Reuven Baron, the illustrious masseur and to everyone who was there for me. Without you, I wouldn't have been able to maintain my sanity during the treatment, and certainly not see and experience things from a different perspective.

- To my oncologists, the amazing Dr. Alona Zer, for accompanying me all through the period of my sickness with endless devotion and concern continuing up to this day, and the unique and dedicated Dr. Daniel Hendler, for your treatment and concern during this difficult period, and for always being there for me personally and professionally.

- To Dr. Eliahu Perlov and Tamar Kadosh, for teaching me the meaning of humanity and for granting me enormous mental strength.

- To Dr. Shlomit Perry, Director of the Social Work Services of the Davidoff Center, Beilinson, for listening and accepting, and for your immense support.
- To my amazing psychologist, Ziva Oded, for being there for me with dedication and humanity during the period of my sickness, for understanding my pain and dilemmas, and for helping me cure the wound in my heart.
- To Jonathan Kedem, spiritual guide and dear friend, for reminding me continuously that there was absolutely no doubt that I'd recover, and for constantly pushing my work forward and believing in me.
- To Nurit Burstein Nevo, for your amazing treatments in Theta Healing and to Galit Pereg, an expert in emotional treatment regarding health and medical issues. Your dedicated treatment helped me release burdens and barriers hidden deep inside me and cleaned the cells in my body and soul.
- To the Press Relations Department of Beilinson Hospital, headed by Vered Kwittel and Liat Hasson: without you I wouldn't have been able to film during my sickness and make my story known worldwide. Your support and your belief in me, your caring and concern, are an integral part of my ability to pass on my impressions to other people.
- To all the rest of the teams and employees of Beilinson Hospital who have not been mentioned here: each and every one of you is personally responsible for my being in this world.

- To Gil Oliamperl and to all the people in the Sabres Group: for me you were the home that provided me with my peace of mind, love and the possibility of earning a living after my recovery and return to regular life.

- To the amazing Zohar and Yankale Yaacobson, the founders of the Tal Center for Integrative Medicine, which gives support to so many sick people! Thank you for your huge support and for being in my life, for your faith, and for pushing forward and putting your soul into each of my projects. You are my guides.

- To Lenny Ravich, a friend, a second father, a great creator, who inspires and guides me in everything I undertake in life. Lenny, you are a role model and a great man full of optimism and humor.

- To my partner Avi Liran, an intellectual and dear friend: thanks to your support, I started my "English journey."

- To the late Bilha Feldman, a rare woman who, though she didn't know it, was the source of my study and my spiritual guide before starting treatment during my sickness.

- To Vered Feldman, my beloved friend: simply – thank you for who and what you are.

- To dear Yoram Levinstein, in whose Studio of Acting I learned to be an actor and artist, who simply turned his studio into a "war room" during my sickness and recruited all the students to collect donations for me during the fundraiser that enabled me to survive that period. I'll never forget this. You are a unique man, one who never abandons his pupils.

- To Tzofit Grant: thank you for your support from the first moment and for your amazing suggestion that I film the entire period of the sickness. Because of you, I had a friend beside me that helped me pour out my heart and recover.
- Thank you, dear readers!!! – for taking some of your precious time to read my book. I sincerely hope you enjoyed it and benefited by it.
- And a last thanks to myself, for agreeing to go through this procedure, fully believing that there is always something new to learn, and for the understanding that this period was just a little obstacle in life and part of something great and empowering. I found the courage to open up, to share my experiences with the world, to develop and grow stronger.

Thanks to this process, I know today that I can't save the world as I always hoped to, but at least I'll die in the knowledge that, every day, I did what I could to influence it for the better and make it a better place.

Made in the USA
Coppell, TX
17 May 2024

32524582R00095